Development in Rich and Poor Countries

Thorkil Kristensen

The Praeger Special Studies program—
utilizing the most modern and efficient book
production techniques and a selective
worldwide distribution network—makes
available to the academic, government, and
business communities significant, timely
research in U.S. and international economic, social, and political development.

Development in Rich and Poor Countries

A General Theory with Statistical Analyses

Praeger Publishers   New York   Washington   London

Praeger Special Studies in International Economics and Development

Library of Congress Cataloging in Publication Data

Kristensen, Thorkil, 1899-
    Development in rich and poor countries.

    (Praeger special studies in international economics
and development)
    Includes bibliographical references.
    1. Economic development.   I. Title.
HD82.K75   309.2'3   73-21467
ISBN 0-275-08690-9

PRAEGER PUBLISHERS
111 Fourth Avenue, New York, N.Y. 10003, U.S.A.
5, Cromwell Place, London SW7 2JL, England

Published in the United States of America in 1974
by Praeger Publishers, Inc.

Printed in the United States of America

PREFACE

This book has been written because I became convinced there was a need for a more comprehensive approach to the study of development than that which we have had until now. We should study the process of development as it goes on in all kinds of countries, whether they are rich or poor and whether their political systems are socialistic or capitalistic. The problems of the so-called developing countries can only be understood in a reasonably satisfactory way as integral parts of a more general theory of the development of human societies.

Such a theory would include the economic, social, political, and cultural aspects of the development process. It would take into account the factors determining population development and the economic and political relationships among national states, as well as the interaction between man and the natural environment. It would therefore require a multidisciplinary approach that involves many branches of modern science.

It is obvious that no one person can produce such a general theory; this book is nothing more than an attempt to make a step towards the broadening of social studies that we need in order to understand the difficult phase of history through which we are going.

Two other leading ideas have guided the work on this study. The first is that the advance of knowledge has contributed more to the change and development of human societies than any other single factor, and that it still does. The role of knowledge in the development process should therefore be given a more important place in the study of that process than has usually been the case. Secondly, it is now possible to undertake an empirical, comparative study of the development process in all countries by means of statistical information published by the international organizations. Therefore the book contains a large number of tables illustrating various aspects of the development process. Work on these tables has widened my own understanding of a number of problems, and I hope the readers of the book will have a similar experience.

Those who want to get a quick impression of the main lines of thought guiding the study may start by reading the Introduction, Chapter 8, and the last section of Chapter 9.

My thanks are due to the Danish Council on Social Research for an appropriation in support of the work, and to my former colleagues in the Institute for Development Research in Copenhagen for the fruitful discussions we have had on problems dealt with in the book. Else Kristensen, M.S., has helped me with a number of publications concerning food production and thereby widened my understanding of its natural science aspects.

T. K.

Copenhagen
March 1974

CONTENTS

LIST OF TABLES AND FIGURES

INTRODUCTION

Much has been written in recent years about development and about the problems of the so-called developing countries. No doubt there is a better understanding now than twenty years ago of what is often called the development process; yet it is probably true that there is a need for a more comprehensive approach.

When a student of a certain discipline deals with development he is bound to concentrate on those aspects of it in which his competance lies; this has often been done by the students of a number of disciplines. Not often, however, have the contributions of the various disciplines been combined in a really comprehensive study. We are therefore far from having what might be called a general theory of development of human societies.

If we are to move in the direction of such a theory based on today's knowledge in various fields, we will no doubt have to employ a multidisciplinary approach. This is so because development is a multidimensional process. Changes are taking place in such factors as income levels, methods of production, health conditions, political systems, and relations with the natural environment; these changes are all interrelated in ways that no single branch of social or natural science can describe adequately.

Students of various disciplines will therefore have to be involved, and they must to some extent learn to understand one another's language. Part of the approach will, however, consist of an exchange of questions and answers between disciplines. Those who work in a certain branch of science will soon find that their own analysis can only throw light on some aspects of the development process, and they will at various points find that questions have been raised that require a different kind of analysis from theirs. Students from other lines of research will then take over and see if they can throw light on other aspects of that complex system of interaction of many factors that we call the development process.

A general theory of development would be much more than a theory of economic growth. It would deal with *both* economic, social, cultural, and political aspects of development, as well as with the relationship between man and the environment. It would, however, be less than a theory of history. World history is a unique, irreversible process, and opinions vary about how meaningful generalizations about its course through the ages can be.

It would be a more modest undertaking to study the development process as it is going on in various kinds of human societies during the present phase of history, in which for the first time nearly all parts of the earth are organized as sovereign states, and in which nearly all governments are concerned about the development of their countries in a relatively broad sense. To the extent that regularities, even if imperfect, are found in the development process of today it may help us to get a somewhat fuller understanding of our own age and also to get some ideas about possible courses of development in what is sometimes called the foreseeable future.

It is the purpose of this book to make a contribution to the building up of a general theory of development in this comprehensive sense. Being an economist and former politician, I am aware that even the economic and political aspects of development can only be understood well by drawing on disciplines other than economics and political science, and I have tried to do so to the best of my ability. The result is bound to be imperfect, but making the study of development more multidisciplinary than it usually is must in itself be considered a high priority at the present juncture.

Apart from this general consideration the study has been guided by some leading ideas resulting from my work on development problems over a number of years. The most important are the five ideas following:

1. A theory of development should deal with societies at all economic levels, and not just with so-called developing countries. All countries are developing, in fact, even the richest ones, and economic and political relations between more and less rich or powerful nations are important aspects of the development process.

2. Knowledge should be given a more prominent and independent place as a factor of production and development than it usually has had in economic theory and development theory. Through the ages the growth of the stock of knowledge has been more important than any other factor leading to change in human societies. Looking at the world today, we find that the most decisive difference between what we call more and less developed countries is that the former are able to apply modern knowledge to a larger extent than the latter. This is why the more developed countries are richer. It is therefore a major aim of the poorer countries to have more and more of this knowledge applied to their various activities in order to reach higher economic levels.

3. It follows from this that it is misleading to talk about developed and developing countries, as is often done. No country is fully developed, since no country can have applied all of the possible knowledge to all its activities.

In fact it is often more meaningful to distinguish among three categories of countries than between two. In this study I shall as a rule make use of the following three categories:

High Income Countries (HICs)*
Medium Income Countries (MICs)
Low Income Countries (LICs)

In Chapter 4 it will be demonstrated that, generally speaking, MICs have the fastest economic growth. The reason for this is that these countries have attained a position in which they are able to adopt modern techniques on a

---

*These abbreviations will be used throughout the book.

large scale. Japan and a few other countries have done this in a remarkable way since World War II, but the same is true to a considerable extent of most MICs.

The two other categories of countries have a slower economic growth, but for very different reasons. HICs are already applying modern knowledge to most of their activities, while LICs do not yet have the strength to adopt highly productive techniques to any large extent.

It will appear from Chapters 5 through 7 that the rapid economic growth of MICs is accompanied by other changes that in a more general way reflect a profound transformation of their societies. There are therefore good reasons why they should be treated as a separate category.

4. We have now reached a stage at which theoretical considerations can be supported by the analysis of a rather comprehensive mass of statistical information. In this study a systematic effort has been made to analyze the statistics of international organizations regarding some major aspects of development. As a general rule, statistics from the United Nations family of organizations have been chosen because they cover countries at all income levels and because they present the figures in a way that makes them comparable between countries.

In most cases the statistical analysis has been confined to the decade from 1960 to 1970 because this is the first decade for which statistics are relatively abundant. It is also the first period in which nearly all countries have been independent and in which they have been pursuing deliberate policies favoring development. In a few cases it has been possible to include figures for the 1950s and the early part of the 1970s as well.

In order not to make the text too difficult to read, all technical comments on the statistical tables are assembled in an annex.

5. Explicitly or implicitly, most scientific research is undertaken in the hope that it may help us to get some ideas about the future, about how things may develop and how we might influence their course.

This is done explicitly in Chapter 9. In the last section of that chapter a few policy issues are discussed, and I have found that some reflexions on possible future trends are a useful background for such a policy discussion. At the same time these reflexions may throw new light on the analysis of past development contained in the book as a whole.

A modern historian has said that what historians think about the past is influenced by their ideas about the future. He was probably right, but I think the opposite is equally true. Therefore, what is said in Chapter 9 is closely related to the analysis in the previous chapters.

One final question must be dealt with by way of introduction, namely that of definitions, since much confusion in the literature stems from the fact that authors often talk about development without making it clear what they mean. It seems appropriate to start by asking the question, What do we want a theory of development to explain? The answer is threefold.

1. We obviously want it to explain, to the extent possible, the changes that take place in the structure of human societies. The question can be asked, however, whether it should be limited to steps forward or upward or in some other sense denoting progress or improvement. I think there should be no such limitation; any change in the structure of society is of interest. It is no less important to understand changes that we consider unfavorable than to

understand those that are more favorable. Furthermore, changes that appear to represent progress may contain the germs of a decline that we will not notice until a later stage.

Development in general should therefore be defined as any structural change in a human society. The adjective "structural" seems to be essential to avoid including the changes that take place all the time, such as that some people die while others are born; and one year the weather is favorable to human life while the next year it may be bad. Such changes need not concern us here if the structure of the society in question remains, roughly speaking, unchanged. If the size and age composition of the population, the nature of its activities, and the relations between persons and groups remain virtually what they used to be, there is nothing for a theory of development to explain.

Such societies do in fact exist. There are still a few, one might say pre-agricultural, societies where no substantial changes of a structural nature seem to take place; this book therefore, does not deal with them. It deals with societies that have an agricultural base, plus some more or less important nonagricultural activities. In such societies, today including the vast majority of human beings, structural changes seem to go on almost without interruption, although slowly in some cases. They are therefore developing, in the general sense of the word, as used here, and a general theory of development should deal with all of the kinds of structural change taking place in them whether the changes are good or bad.

2. This does not mean it is unimportant whether development is good or bad. For this we need two supplementary definitions: by "positive development" I shall understand any structural change that represents a step forward or an improvement; by "negative development" is understood a deterioration or a step backwards.

In contrast to the general definition given above, these two concepts are obviously value-laden. Value judgments are no doubt unavoidable in any serious treatment of development problems, but to make the presentation as clear as possible an author ought to give at least a rough indication of the value premises on which his evaluations are based.

No short statement on such an important question can be quite satisfactory. As a general principle I shall, however, consider changes as positive that increase the harmony in human societies, and as negative those that increase disharmony.

More will be said about harmony and disharmony in Chapter 8. In a preliminary way let it be said that in my view the most dangerous feature of world development today is that it is disharmonious in many respects: there is much inequality of incomes within and still more between national states; there is often a lack of understanding between generations; and there is an ecological disharmony in the pollution and exhaustion of some resources, disturbing our relationship with the natural environment.

One might ask whether harmony is always and under all circumstances something to be welcomed; can it not give us a boring society in which there is too little challenge for the individual? However that may be it does not seem to be a major problem at the present juncture. At least it appears to me that right now there is more reason to fear too much disharmony.

It remains to be noted that since development is a multidimensional process, in a certain period for a given society some elements of it will be considered positive while others are thought to be negative. Whether development as a whole is considered to be positive or negative in such a case is of course a matter for anybody's judgment. There is no way to obtain an objective standard of measurement independent of human value premises.

3. The three definitions given above leave one question unanswered that it seems necessary to consider. In the literature about development we meet again and again expressions like "more and less developed countries," "advanced countries," "underdeveloped countries," and similar descriptions of stages of development.

Such language seems to imply that development is a process that, normally, at least, goes in a certain direction and that a country can only have advanced more or less in that direction. The question is therefore whether there is something that can be called the "typical development process." If there is, all countries, or at least most countries, can be supposed to be going through some stage of that process, although perhaps with considerable variations in specific details.

One of the purposes of the present essay is to throw some light on this question. The subject is dealt with especially in Chapters 4 through 7. In a preliminary way it can be stated that a certain degree of regularity can be found in the processes going on. For instance, in the present phase of world history most countries show some increase in gross national product per capita. Most countries also have declining percentages of their populations engaged in agriculture. In many countries population growth will be influenced for some time by falling death rates because of better health conditions and later on by falling birth rates.

It may be more difficult to generalize about other aspects of the processes of development. It seems that in the course of development income distribution often becomes more unequal up to a point and then more equal, but there may perhaps be more ups and downs; here there is probably a systematic difference between socialist countries and other countries. It follows that expressions like "more developed" and "less developed" should be used with great care. If a country has a slightly higher average level of income than another, but a more unequal distribution, which one is the most developed? If it is thought necessary to use "more developed" and "less developed"—and often it may be unavoidable—some clarity can be provided by adding adjectives like "economically" and "socially."

In conclusion a few words should be said about each of the chapters of this book.

Chapter 1 deals with the desires and aspirations that have motivated all the efforts leading to structural change in human societies.

Chapter 2 discusses the instruments people have used in these efforts. Of the four factors of production—land, labor, capital, and knowledge—the two former were there from the beginning, while capital and knowledge have been added through human effort. Capital and knowledge are therefore the true factors of development, and it is argued that knowledge is the most decisive of the two. One might say that advance in knowledge is the active factor of development. Capital is accumulated in order to make the application of more and more knowledge possible.

Chapter 3 deals with innovation, the process by which more and more knowledge is applied to human activities. A note at the end of the chapter outlines a few major features of the course of innovation throughout history.

The next four chapters contain the statistical analysis indicated above. Chapter 4 describes economic development. It is here that the three categories, HIC, MIC, and LIC, are introduced and combined with the regional comparisons frequently made in development studies.

Chapter 5 deals with a number of indicators of social development, and is therefore a necessary supplement to the economic analysis in Chapter 4. It also contains sections on cultural and political development, which can be considered parts of social development in a wider sense.

Chapter 6 deals with the development of population, which in this study is considered to be closely related to the economic and social development treated in the two previous chapters and also to motivation, which is treated in Chapter 1. I think population development has been studied too much in isolation and too little as an integral part of the development process.

Chapter 7 deals with economic and other relations between the national states that are the main actors on the world scene of development today.

Chapter 8 draws some general conclusions from the analysis of the previous chapters and discusses the extent to which it is meaningful to talk about the typical development process.

Chapter 9, finally, deals with the future in the way indicated above.

Development in Rich and Poor Countries

1

MOTIVATION

Human beings have in common with all animals an instinctive inclination to seek food and other necessities. In addition, we have developed over the ages a more or less conscious desire to influence things around us in ways that bring them closer to the goals or intentions we may have. One of our goals has probably always been a desire to improve the material conditions of life, but increasingly other goals have been added.

This desire has been the motive-power behind the development of human societies. The extent to which it has been present has varied much from one society to another and also from one period to another within the same society. Apparantly it has been weak and even nearly absent over long periods in some societies that have remained in about the same situation for centuries. It is an intriguing question, whether these societies have stagnated because of a weak desire for change or whether no strong wish to improve the conditions of life could develop because the environment did not appear favorable to such improvement. This question shall not be discussed further in this book, but it is worth remembering that one of the strongest obstacles to the start of a development process in a hitherto stagnant society may well be this lack of motivation for change.

In other societies the motivating forces have been stronger and have led to actions that have gradually changed the patterns of social life. As a rule what we call the development process has made these patterns more sophisticated and created more and more complex systems of rural and urban communities, linked together through increasingly numerous transactions.

During this process there have been important interactions between the motives of individuals and the development of society brought about by the actions resulting from these motives. Motives are influenced by living conditions. Quite naturally someone who is living in a big modern city and enjoying a comfortable life has different ways of thinking and therefore different motives for action from those of a subsistence farmer in an isolated village in a poor country.

If there is a general trend in the changes human motives have undergone during the process of development, it is a trend towards extension in two dimensions. First, one can speak of a "deepening," in the sense that the simple desire for more food and other material goods is gradually being transformed into a desire for ways of life that give a fuller satisfaction to the aspirations of man. Thus has developed the wish to possess and to create beautiful things, the desire for more knowledge and understanding of the world, and sometimes the desire to develop the physical, mental, and moral capacities of the individual. An increasing understanding of the world and of the nature of human society should normally sharpen the moral consciousness because it makes one more aware of the consequences of one's own actions.

Second, at the same time a "widening" of the desire for improvement takes place. In the early stages it hardly goes beyond the family in the narrowest sense, but with the development of even larger societies it can comprise the enlarged family, the tribe, the nation, and even mankind as a whole. Much has been said about the insufficiency of the present flow of aid to the less developed countries, but it is significant that such aid has now become a regular part of the policies of rich countries. This demonstrates that the feeling of human solidarity is beginning to transcend national frontiers. We are slowly realizing that the only natural subject of human solidarity is humanity as a whole.

However, the transformation of human motives is a very complex process. Apart from the deepening and widening mentioned above, one could perhaps talk about a third dimension of these motives, namely a desire to improve one's position, compared with and sometimes even at the expense of that of other people.

As long as this is only a wish to obtain prestige and the admiration of other people its main effect may be to encourage a more excellent performance. It can, however, develop into greed for excessive wealth or power on one's own behalf or on behalf of one's family or country, and in that case it can often lead to actions of a destructive nature.

In this respect it is important to note that when some people or groups are more powerful than others it will be their motives that have the strongest impact on the development of society. In most societies there has probably been a dominating class or caste, such as the big landowners, the clergy, or the military, that has been particularly powerful over long periods. In other cases much power has been invested in a dictator or in the leaders of a ruling political party. Appetite comes from eating, and powerful people are often eager to get more power. Even fear can further such a desire for power when one feels that one's position is threatened by the growing power of other people or other countries.

These particular kinds of motivation have to do with the fact that men and women live in groups. In modern societies a person can belong to a number of groups, such as a family, a class, a political party, and a nation. This of course complicates every individual's situation.

The study of various animals living in groups has disclosed some striking similarities between their patterns of behavior and those of human beings. There is often a strong solidarity within the group, combined with a defensive attitude toward other groups. This can turn into aggression when one group tries to penetrate another group's territory. That a group or even a single couple can consider a certain territory as its own and therefore be ready to defend it is well known of many species of animals. In spite of this group solidarity there may be competition for the leadership. Often an old animal is the obvious leader, but collective leadership is not unknown, and there are cases where a real hierarchy exists.

All these features, of course, can be found in human societies as well. The difference is that while they have a hereditary and instinctive character on the part of animals they have increasingly become conscious on the part of men and women. This means that increasingly a person reflects before acting and therefore can take into account the knowledge gathered throughout a lifetime.

As usual, knowledge is for good and evil. Knowledge about possible consequences can make a person abstain from action, but it can also make an aggressive act more sophisticated and therefore more destructive.

It will be argued in the following chapters that advances in knowledge have been the most powerful factor of development throughout history, and that they still are. This is so not only because more knowledge helps us to work more effectively for the goals we already have, but also because advances in knowledge influence our goals by enabling us to see them in a wider perspective.

This influence of new knowledge on our system of motivation may be said to come through an awareness of something new, but it may also come from an awareness of something that has existed for years without being brought to our attention in a sufficiently forceful way.

An example will illustrate this. Formerly people used to have many children, partly at least because infant mortality was so high that only a few of the children survived. Now infant mortality has gone down drastically even in most LICs, but the birth rates are still high because the people are not sufficiently aware of the new situation.

It can be important to increase people's (including governments') awareness of many aspects of current development that everybody would agree to call dangerous if sufficient thought were given to them. Reference will be made to such cases in the following chapters.

2

FACTORS OF DEVELOPMENT

FACTORS OF PRODUCTION

In most societies simple food gathering has long ago been replaced by more systematic efforts to make food and other desired things available for consumption. It has been replaced by the production of goods and services, including transportation and distribution, that now occupy most people most of their time. The results of production and the ways in which it is organized are therefore important aspects of development.

The factors that, combined, result in the total production can be classified in various ways. No classification can claim to be considered the only valid one, nor even the most suitable for all purposes. It depends on the specific nature of a study, which system of classification is most appropriate.

For reasons explained below it seems convenient for many purposes to distinguish between four factors of production: land, labor, capital, and knowledge. By "land" I shall understand all natural resources in and below the soil, including mineral deposits, forests, rivers, lakes, and oceans, to the extent they are useful to human beings. By "labor" is understood any human effort made in the production of goods and services. "Capital" includes all of the material means of production that have themselves been produced, such as tools, machinery, buildings, livestock, ships, and other means of transportation and communication. Under the term *knowledge* I shall include any knowledge gained through practical experience or through scientific research or any other kind of experimental activity.

Land and labor were available from the beginning of human life on earth. What has been added through the ages is more and more capital and knowledge, and this is what has increased the productivity of both land and labor. Capital and knowledge therefore are the true factors of development.

Land is particularly important in the early stages of development because there is so little capital and knowledge. Countries that are amply endowed with natural resources are therefore often considerably more wealthy than other countries at a similar level of technical development. Some oil-producing countries are conspicuous examples of this.

On the other hand, with increasing investments of capital and knowledge in the production process, the relative importance of land decreases. Switzerland has one of the highest income levels in the world, although it does not have much agricultural land or other natural resources per capita.

Knowledge is not usually treated by economists as a factor of production in the same way as land, labor, and capital. Sometimes it is described as intellectual capital, as distinct from the material objects included in the normal concept of capital. There is, however, an increasing tendency to take knowledge, or the level of knowledge, into account in the analysis in one way or another.

There are indeed similarities between capital and knowledge. Both are man-made. They are means of production that have themselves been produced. Both can also be considered as investments; that is, as results of production set aside for use in the future, as opposed to consumption goods, which disappear as such when consumed.

Both capital and knowledge become obsolete when better capital objects and more perfect knowledge become available. Capital objects are subject to depreciation, both because they can be worn out and because of obsolescence. Similarly, knowledge can be forgotten, which is a reason why much education in poor countries is wasted. A child who has been to school for one or two years, which is not unusual, may be virtually illiterate when grown up. When a house burns, the capital invested in it is lost. The same is true of the knowledge invested in a man, when he dies.

There are, however, also important dissimilarities between knowledge and capital. Knowledge is in principle everlasting. The particular knowledge belonging to a man disappears at his death but our knowledge about electricity or atomic energy will rest with mankind. It can be replaced by more perfect knowledge about these phenomena, as capital can be replaced by more perfect capital, but it is not subject to wear and tear.

The importance of this fact was demonstrated in a remarkable way after World War II. Countries like Western Germany and Japan had a lot of material capital destroyed during the war, but both had a remarkable economic recovery afterwards. Knowledge had been preserved and had even expanded, so that new capital could be invested at a higher level of technical knowledge.

This fact reflects another quality that is peculiar to knowledge. In contrast to the three other factors of production, it has in principle an unlimited capacity. A ship or a factory can transport or produce limited quantities of goods during a limited period, but a new method of production can be used to make unlimited quantities of the goods in question as long as desired. In other words, knowledge has a "multiplication effect" that no other factor of production possesses.

At this point it may be appropriate to make a few comments on the interaction between knowledge and capital in production and thereby also in development. Knowledge has been the dynamic, or active, factor in the development of more and more efficient methods of production, while capital has been the passive factor needed for the utilization of knowledge. Accumulation of capital has been important because it has helped man to apply an increasing stock of knowledge, but the large capital formation of modern societies would make no sense without the unique expansion of knowledge during the last century. It is in order to utilize this knowledge in the production of numerous new goods, from foodstuffs to airplanes, that a great deal more capital has been needed than in earlier times.

For similar reasons, the poorer countries need more knowledge adapted to their situation, even more than they need capital, since without adequate knowledge they would not be able to utilize more capital. This is all the more important because the difference between these countries and the richer ones is greater regarding knowledge than regarding capital. It has been estimated that about 10 percent of the world's capital formation, but only about 2 percent of its scientific research, takes place in the so-called developing countries. More will be said about these important aspects of development in the following chapters.

Also, the expansion of knowledge has been more important for the world as a whole than any other factor in the development process, as indicated in the above description of its interaction with capital formation. In a way this expansion can also be characterized as the most lasting effect of the development process. Opinions may differ widely about whether the world is making progress in the sense of becoming better, but there can be no doubt that the stock of knowledge is larger than ever before. Nor does it seem questionable that knowledge will continue to grow rather fast in the foreseeable future. Whether there is an ultimate limit to the level the stock of knowledge can attain or not, it seems evident that for a long time to come each generation will have more knowledge than its predecessors.

Because of the crucial importance of the expansion of knowledge it may be appropriate to take a look at the ways in which knowledge expands. It does in fact expand in two directions. I shall speak of expansion in "depth" when more knowledge is added to that already existing, to give us a deeper understanding of the world or of any theoretical or practical problem. Expansion in "breadth" takes place when the same knowledge spreads to more people.

Looking first at expansion in depth I shall begin by defining what I call "the existing knowledge" at a given moment. It consists of any knowledge about any subject existing anywhere in the world. This is a kind of fund, in principle available to mankind, although there may be obstacles to the spreading of parts of it for a shorter or longer period. It is conceivable that at a given moment, parts of the existing knowledge are in fact the knowledge of nobody. They may exist only in written form, such as notes left by a scientist when he dies. The knowledge is existing, nevertheless, and it can be spread when it is found and multiplied.

How does knowledge expand in depth? We may get knowledge about something that was unknown before, but more often our knowledge expands by becoming what we now consider better or more correct.

What we call knowledge is in fact only a series of imperfect pictures of the world or parts of it. Advances in knowledge therefore usually do not mean simply that wrong opinions are replaced by right ones, but rather that imperfect pictures are replaced by new pictures. These, though also imperfect, are considered more satisfactory than the former ones.

Practically speaking, this normally means that they help us to solve technical, administrative, or other problems in what we consider more efficient ways. From a theoretical point of view, it often means that we get a fuller understanding by discovering that a certain phenomenon can be seen as an integral part of a larger system, composed of many interacting parts.

The most spectacular example of this, of course, is our ever-expanding picture of the universe. The same principles, however, apply to the development process. To a rather simple theory of economic growth is gradually added ever more considerations about the social, cultural, political, and environmental aspects of the structural changes going on in human societies.

Expansion of knowledge in breadth, while a similar affair than its expansion in depth, is also a field in which rapid technological progress has taken place. Modern means of communication permit any kind of information to be spread all over the world in a moment. It is through education and training that knowledge really becomes the property of men and women, however. With the steady increase in existing knowledge, the way education is organized becomes an important policy issue in all countries. This is particularly true in the poorer countries, where an increase in knowledge, as already indicated, is even more important than an increase in the supply of capital. This problem will be discussed further in Chapters 5 and 9.

THE DOMINANT FACTOR

In societies where agriculture is the main activity, land is the dominant factor of production. Ownership of land therefore becomes an important source of income, and if much land is owned by the same person it will also easily become a source of power. In predominantly agricultural societies the big landowners have often been the politically dominating class, the more so because most of the farmers have been tenants or even serfs and therefore dependent on the landowners. This system of feudalism was dominant in European countries until the 18th or 19th century.

With the growing importance of commerce and shipping, and even more with the development of mechanized industry, capital began to replace land as the dominant factor of production in many countries, and at the same time a new class of industrial workers began to appear, replacing the artisans of former times. The new class became dependent on the owners of the new enterprises, in a way that sometimes exposed them to miserable conditions of life. The owners of capital now assumed position that in some respects can be compared with that of the landlords under feudalism.

It is, therefore, no accident that the word "capitalism" became attached in particular to the emerging system of privately owned industrial enterprises. The contrast between the wealth of the "captains of industry" and the miserable situation of much of the new working class was an understandable background of the various socialistic philosophies that emerged in this period.

However, an increase in the quantity of one factor of production will, other things being equal, increase the productivity of the others, while the marginal productivity of the growing factor will fall. Further accumulation of capital thus increases the productivity of labor and thereby contributes to a subsequent rise in real wages. A study of development in Sweden from 1908 to 1938[1] has shown that during that period real capital doubled in quantity, while the labor force increased by only 35 percent. As a consequence the productivity of labor increased so much that labor income in 1938 represented five-sixths of the national income, compared with two-thirds in 1908, while capital income represented one-sixth, compared with one-third, and the average rate of interest fell from 6 to 4 percent.

In this way the wide gap between the capitalists and the workers of early industrial Western Europe was gradually modified, a development that Auguste Comte, in contrast to Karl Marx, had foreseen.[2] This is why the Marxist revolution did not take place in Western Europe, where its philosophy had originated, but rather in Russia and China, which came into the 20th century with the sharp contrasts of early capitalism and even feudalism still existing.

A new development has come about with the explosive growth of knowledge in the present century. Progressively, knowledge is replacing capital as the dominant factor. The fact that knowledge plays an increasing role is confirmed by some estimates made by Theodore W. Schultz,[3] who calculated the amounts invested in physical capital and in education during the years 1929-57 in the United States. The results are as follows:

	Physical Capital	Education
Annual growth, 1929-57 (per cent)	2.01	3.57
Total investment, 1957 (in billions of dollars)	1,270	848

If to education we add research, information activity, and other forms of "production of knowledge," it seems likely in view of the trends that the total investment in knowledge is now larger than the investment in physical means of production, and it is increasing much faster. This confirms the impression that at least the most economically developed countries are moving towards or have reached a situation in which knowledge replaces capital as the most important factor of production.

An effort to measure the contributions of the various factors to the increase in total production over a certain period has been made by Edward E. Denison, who traced the growth of production in the United States in the years 1929-57.[4] The annual growth of the gross national product was 2.93 percent, and the contributions of the individual factors to this growth were estimated to be the following:

	Contribution (percent)
Quantity of labor (by hours)	.80
Quantity of capital	.43
Education and experience	.77
Advance of knowledge	.59
Other factors	.34

The contribution of more education and experience corresponds to what is called "knowledge embodied in man." What Denison calls "advance of knowledge" is mainly the use of more advanced technology and business methods. Together with education and experience it is therefore part of the factor knowledge. This means that according to Denison's estimate the increase in knowledge has been responsible for an annual growth of production of 1.36 percent, compared with .80 percent for the increase of labor and .43 percent for the increase of capital. Of course, much of the revenue from the increase in knowledge goes to people who have more knowledge than others. The differences in earnings between white-collar employees, skilled workers, and unskilled workers are, roughly speaking, payments for knowledge. The "other factors" mentioned in the table include the advantages of production on a larger scale in 1957 than in 1929. Partly this is also a result of increases in knowledge.

Denison also made some calculations for the period 1909-29. The information concerning those years is less complete, but it is clear from the comparisons made, that knowledge plays a larger role in the years 1929-57 than in the earlier period.

KNOWLEDGE AND SOCIAL CHANGE

Not only has knowledge become the dominant factor of production in those HICs in which its level is the highest, but in a wider sense it has also strongly influenced the social, cultural, and even political patterns of modern high income societies. In due course it can be expected to have a similar influence on societies where the level of knowledge is now lower.

It was mentioned above that the advantages of modern large-scale production result partly from increases in knowledge. This is because of the unlimited capacity of knowledge referred to earlier. If a factory becomes too big, transportation within it and between the factory and parts of its market becomes too costly. But an enterprise can have 100 factories in 50 countries, and the costs of research and development (that is, of knowledge) will be much lower per unit produced than if there were only one factory. Also, modern means of communication make it easier than before to manage a large number of factories in many countries as integral parts of one enterprise.

The same is true of advances in financial techniques, an important part of modern knowledge. The development of the banking system and of corporations has made it possible to concentrate investment of capital in large enterprises, while the ownership of that capital may be spread over many thousands of stockholders and bank depositors.

Taken together, these new trends in the development of knowledge have had two important social consequences. One is reduction of the power of the owners of large amounts of capital. Since capital can now be got on the market through borrowing and the issuing of stocks, one does not need to be a multimillionaire to create a large enterprise. The other is the creation of a big hierarchy within such an enterprise. In such a hierarchy the position of people increasingly depends on their competence, more than on their ownership of capital. The same is true in public administration and in scientific and other institutions of a semipublic nature that are important elements of the infrastructure of modern societies.

These new developments are illustrations of the fact already mentioned, that knowledge is now replacing capital as the dominant factor in HICs and increasingly also in other countries.

There are in fact clear signs in several countries that those who are in leading positions by virtue of their competence are becoming a kind of "knowledge aristocracy," which has replaced the landowning and capitalist aristocracies of former times. The Cultural Revolution in China was partly an effort to avoid such a development.

We are thus moving into what has been called The Knowledge Society.[5] There is an important difference, though, between this and the earlier feudal and capitalist societies: land and capital could be accumulated in large quantities by a single owner, who could own many times as much as the ordinary man, who might possess next to nothing.

Knowledge cannot be accumulated to the same extent. The brain of even the brightest person has a limited capacity, and his intelligence is not necessarily inherited by his children as was the land and the capital of the aristocrats of former times.

It is important to stress this because one of the problems of the future is to what extent the LICs, especially, can bypass the feudalist and the capitalist phases in their development and thus move directly towards a knowledge society, where inequalities are less brutal. More will be said about this in Chapter 9.

It is, by the way, likely that the present power of the knowledge aristocracy will gradually diminish as the general standard of knowledge is increased, in the same way that the power of the capitalists culminated in the early phases of industrial capitalism. It is understandable that the socialist way of thinking appeared in that period, and similarly, there is now a certain reaction against the power of the knowledge aristocracy, not only in China.

The gradual spread of knowledge has had other consequences. There is a growing breakdown of traditional ways of thinking, a tendency not to simply accept that what one's parents believed is right. Almost everything is now questioned, including inherited religious, political, and cultural creeds. In a sense one can speak of a cultural revolution in other countries as well as China.

This has created much uncertainty in many HICs. It is, of course, easier to criticize traditional values than to formulate clear ideas about the next steps to take.

In one respect the ideas about the next phase are rather clear. There is a growing desire to move towards more equality in rights and in benefits. This includes political democracy and participation in the decision making of the big enterprises and other institutions; it also includes support for independence in territories that still have a colonial status; and it includes the desire to move towards more equality of income within and between national societies. It is only natural that the gradual spread of knowledge in all classes of society should have such consequences.

NOTES

1. F. Zeuthen, *Social Sikring* (Copenhagen: Arnold Busk, 1947), p. 273.

2. Raymond Aron, *Trois Essays sur l'Age Industriel* (Paris: Plon, 1965), p. 27.

3. Theodore W. Schultz, *The Economic Value of Education* (New York: Columbia University Press, 1963), Table 4.

4. Edward E. Denison, *The Residual Factor in Economic Growth* (Paris: OECD, 1964), Table 1.

5. See, for instance, Peter F. Drucker, *The Age of Discontinuity* (London: Heinemann, 1969), Part Four.

3

INNOVATION

THREE TYPES OF INNOVATION

Innovation is the process through which more and more knowledge is applied to human activities. New or different activities are thus created, and this is what provokes structural change in human societies.

One often talks about innovation as something that has to do with economic activity in the narrower sense of production of goods and services for the market. Innovation then means the introduction of new products or new methods of production. It is reasonable, however, to conceive of innovative acts as comprising everything that changes the ways in which human beings do what they do. Innovation in education, in methods of research, or in public administration or political systems can be a powerful instrument of structural change.

Original Innovation

The first step in any innovation is the invention of a new product or a new method of production, education, or whatever it may be. The invention may result from scientific research or from practical experience. It may represent a major breakthrough or just a modest improvement in methods of work.

It may happen that an invention does not lead to any innovation, at least immediately, because it is not found useful or profitable to apply it to human activities. It is well known that certain important inventions have not been put to use until many years after the time they were made because the society in question was not ready for them. It also happens, however, that inventions are translated into innovation in a way that is not suited to further a harmonious development of the society in which it takes place. One of the

14

major problems dealt with in this study is how to direct the process of innovation in such a way that it will serve the various types of society in more appropriate ways than it often does today.

Transferred Innovation

Any innovation must begin somewhere. It is "original innovation" at the enterprise or the institution where it is first developed. From there is spreads and becomes "transferred innovation" in other enterprises and often in other countries. It takes, of course, much more competence and often a much larger input in the form of research and product development to undertake original innovation, than simply to imitate what has already been done elsewhere. Original innovation therefore plays a much greater role in the technically highly developed countries than in those that are less advanced.

This of course is a difference of degree only. Much transfer of innovation takes place even in rich, industrial countries and between such countries. The fact remains, however, that the less developed countries are depending much more on transferred innovation. The tendency for these countries to use techniques already developed by the industrial countries is one of the characteristic features of the present phase of world history. Of course, some competent people and some capital investment are needed at the receiving end, but sometimes these are partly supplied by firms or governments in the rich countries, and at any rate it is a great advantage that the groundwork of original innovation has already been done.

Adaptive Innovation

There is, however, a problem regarding transfer of technology that seems to be of increasing importance at the moment. Very often techniques that have developed in the industrial countries do not meet the needs of the technically less developed nations. There can be various reasons for this.

In agriculture, soil and climate vary greatly from one country to another, and even from one region to another within the same country. Most LICs and many MICs are tropical or subtropical, but nearly all the industrial countries lie in the temperate zone. Therefore the kinds of plants and animals as well as the methods of cultivation and care, must be adapted to the conditions of the country in question. Therefore, besides original and transferred innovation there is a third category that might be called adaptive innovation. As a rule it is a mixture of transferred and original innovation. An example may serve as an illustration.

When a new high-yield strain of Mexican wheat was introduced into Turkey, it was discovered to be less resistant to certain diseases than traditional Turkish wheat. Research is therefore going on in Turkey in order to develop crossbreeds that are both resistant and high-yielding. This research is original insofar as nothing exactly like it has been done before, but of course it profits from the experience gained through the research done in Mexico and both profit from the general knowledge about genetics developed by scientists in various countries.

A more general problem of adaptive innovation stems from the fact that modern techniques have developed in countries with abundant and therefore cheap capital, but with labor that was relatively short in supply and therefore expensive. They are therefore usually labor-saving and capital intensive; in fact, both the inputs of capital and of knowledge per man-hour are high. The situation of the poorest countries, however, is exactly the opposite. Capital is scarce and very expensive, while labor is relatively abundant and cheap. In all activities, therefore, it will usually be preferable to have techniques that are labor intensive, but that require simple and cheap items of capital and not too much highly qualified labor.

Such techniques only exist to a very limited extent today. As a result, most low income countries have a "dual economy," wherein a small sector consists of modern, capital-intensive industry while the rest of the community applies traditional labor intensive techniques to agriculture and handicrafts. There is often a wide gap between the income levels in these two sectors.

An important task for innovation in the years to come will be to develop techniques that are capital saving and labor intensive, but nevertheless based on the results of modern science. This will, of course, require close cooperation between scientists and technicians in technically more and less developed countries.

It will also require a considerable innovation in the educational system. Too often less developed countries have tried to imitate the education of the rich countries at all levels, with the result that they have unemployed engineers, and farmers' sons who have gone to school but who do not know the techniques appropriate for agriculture in their own country. There is a need for more adult education that is adapted to the techniques that will have to be developed for agriculture and industry, even at the expense of some slowing down in the expansion of western-type education. Practical vocational training may be placed higher on the priority lists in the years to come. Knowledge, like capital, should be provided in forms that meet the needs of the countries in question.

More will be said about education in Chapters 5, 8, and 9. It is mentioned here in order to illustrate the important fact that adaptive innovation is a two-way traffic. Techniques must be adapted to the circumstances of the society in which they are to be applied. Such transferred and adapted techniques do represent something new, however, especially if they are progressive, leading gradually to higher income level. People in the receiving country should therefore be educated and trained to enable them to undertake tasks that are somewhat different from the traditional ones.

Innovation can change societies gradually and in a fairly harmonious way if it takes place in the form of relatively small steps over a long period. It can also create disharmony, by introducing suddenly or during a short span of years techniques and ways of life that are radically different from the traditional ones. This has often been the case when systems of production, education and government have been transferred from HICs to LICs without sufficient adaptation. A sector is then created in a society in which the majority of the population lives under conditions that are very different from those of the minority benefiting from foreign technology.

Development has been a predominantly continuous process in some countries, while in others important elements of discontinuity have appeared at certain stages. A short historical note should throw some light on the nature and causes of these differences.

INNOVATION IN HISTORY

Some of the countries covered by the present study have gone through a relatively continuous process of innovation for centuries and even millennia. Others have come later into what V. Gordon Childe called "the main stream of human progress,"[1] or they may at some point of time have dropped out of the main stream and perhaps later have joined it again, and so on. The situation of the various countries today is to a large extent determined by the fate they have had in this long historical process.

No attempt is made in this book to formulate a theory of history, but the analysis of recent development that is undertaken in the following chapters should give a fuller understanding of the ongoing changes, especially if it is seen with the help of a short survey, wherein the 122 countries covered by Annex Table 1 are seen in their relations to the "main stream of progress" referred to above.

What does this main stream consist of?

Some historians and archaeologists[2] have described various major break-throughs as revolutions, speaking of "The Agricultural Revolution," "The Urban Revolution," or "The Industrial Revolution," and so on. This language seems appropriate if by revolution we understand, not some violent change of power, but rather a process that might take centuries to be accomplished, but that then leads to a fundamental change of society.

In this sense I shall distinguish six revolutions, covering the last 10,000 years or more: (1) the Agricultural Revolution, (2) the Urban Revolution, (3) the Maritime Revolution, (4) the Scientific Revolution, (5) the Industrial Revolution, and (6) the Egalitarian Revolution. Some of these revolutions seem to have started independently in more than one part of the world. In other cases they have spread from one area to another, or there may have been some interaction between two areas with otherwise independent development. We have thus had a mixture of original and transferred innovation throughout history.

The Agricultural Revolution

The Agricultural Revolution is the process by which simple food gathering was replaced by food production in agriculture and animal husbandry. It seems to have started in various places in West Asia during the period from about 9,000 B.C. to about 7,000 B.C. and somewhat later in various other regions. It is not necessary here to follow this important development in detail, but three features of it are worth mentioning.

The first is that all human societies, with a few exceptions, have gradually gone through the Agricultural Revolution, so that now almost all human beings belong to societies that have an agricultural base.

The second is that, from West Asia where it developed, the first agriculture spread to the major parts of Southern and Western Europe in the period from about 5,000 B.C., thereby creating a basis for the further development of these areas.[3]

The third basic fact about early agricultural societies is that in some places they developed into more sophisticated communities, especially where irrigation had been invented as a means of increasing the output of agriculture. Thus, it has been indicated that the yield of wheat in southern Iraq was remarkably high at an early stage and that this may have been one of the "predisposing conditions" for the growth of the Sumerian civilization.[4]

The Urban Revolution

The Urban Revolution represents a gradual development of some agricultural villages into larger towns and cities, where handicrafts and commerce became separate activities alongside of agriculture. One can therefore speak of the beginning of differentiation of society. This was combined with progress in metallurgy and with such important innovations as the wheel and the art of writing.

Equally important is the fact that the early city dwellers created political systems in which each city was the center of a little city-state. One can even trace the beginning of imperialism back to the oldest urban civilization, that of Sumer[5] in which each city-state tried to get control of others.

The Sumerian civilization developed in the southern part of Mesopotamia in the second half of the fourth millennium B.C. Not much later the Egyptian civilization took shape in the Nile Valley. Both in Egypt and somewhat later in the Indus Valley there seems to have been a mixture of an independent evolution and a certain stimulus-diffusion from Sumer.

This is not the place for further comments on the discussion among archaeologists about the respective roles of independent development and of stimulus-diffusion. Suffice it to say that of the earliest civilizations, those of Mesopotamia and of Egypt seem to have had more intercourse than any of the others. They were the two oldest; the distance between them was relatively short; and the area lying between them was the one where agriculture had developed first. It is therefore no wonder that communication within this area was relatively lively. Nor is it surprising that the countries bordering the eastern part of the Mediterranean were touched by it. Gordon Childe talks about the "formation of the 'main stream'" and has followed "its course from sources in Egypt and Mesopotamia to their confluence in the Hellenistic Mediterranean".[6]

Thus, ancient Greece and later on the Roman Empire became heirs and in some ways successors of the older civilizations of Mesopotamia and Egypt. Further innovation took place. The Greeks developed shipping and the arts and sciences to higher levels, and the Romans created one of the largest and most firmly organized political structures in history.

It is not necessary to follow the evolution through the centuries after the fall of the Roman Empire. It should be mentioned, though, that civilization continued in the Byzantine Empire and in parts of the Arab World, from which it spread to the Iberian Peninsula. Also, a certain development of commerce and banking took place in some Italian cities, and the cathedrals of the late Middle Ages represent remarkable innovations in architecture.

Gradually the leadership passed to Western Europe, where the following "Revolutions" took place. It must suffice to mention them shortly.

The Maritime Revolution

The Maritime Revolution, which means the development of ocean shipping, started in an important way around the year 1500. It represents one of the most far-reaching innovations in history, because for the first time all parts of the earth were brought into communication with one another. It therefore vastly increased the possibilities for international trade and for division of labor among various parts of the world. This gave the occasion for an enormous expansion of colonialism, most parts of the other continents becoming dependent on Western European countries in one way or another.

Indirectly, the Maritime Revolution was one of the preconditions for the Industrial Revolution, which is generally considered as having started in Britain in the 18th century.

The Scientific Revolution

Another precondition for the evolution of modern industry was the Scientific Revolution; that is, the gradual evolution of experimental science, which means, to use the terminology of Chapter 2, that the production of knowledge was undertaken in a much more systematic way than earlier. This process which is still going on, started a little later than the Maritime Revolution. It has enlarged the amount of knowledge available to man, transforming human life at a speed that has been increasing for a long time.

The Industrial Revolution

Fundamentally, therefore, there can hardly be any doubt that the Maritime and the Scientific Revolutions have been more important than the

Industrial Revolution they have engendered. This transformation of the old handicrafts into mechanized industry was made possible through a number of innovations, of which the most important probably was the introduction of new sources of energy such as steam, combustion, electricity, and nuclear fission.

Without the Scientific Revolution these innovations would not have been technically feasible; and without the Maritime Revolution they would not have been economically possible, since neither raw materials and fuel, nor markets for the products would have been available to the extent needed for the expansion of modern industry.

The Egalitarian Revolution

It remains to say a few words about the Egalitarian Revolution. The idea that all men and women should have the same human rights and increasingly equal conditions of life, and that all parts of the earth should have the same right to political sovereignty, is really new and revolutionary. Slavery, serfdom, and colonialism have been well-established features of various older societies, and economic inequality has increased in many countries through important phases of their history.

The American and French revolutions of the 18th century were the first large-scale manifestations of the new movement towards greater political and economic equality. In the centuries before that time there had been a number of peasants' revolts in various countries, but only now were egalitarian ideas gaining enough ground to have political force.

It is probably no accident that this happened in the century after the beginning of the Scientific Revolution. New knowledge leads to new ways of thinking. The old authorities were increasingly being subjected to scrutiny and criticism, and the new ways of thinking were spread by a growing unorthodox literature. The century of the two first great revolutions was also the century of the Enlightenment. It is worth noting that in France as well as in other countries, some of the leading advocates of more freedom and equality belonged to the upper classes.

The Egalitarian Revolution has continued during the 19th and 20th centuries. Political democracy, general suffrage for all men and women, and independence for nearly all the former colonies have been the most spectacular results. Progressive taxation and social security systems have been used as instruments for obtaining more economic equality. At present, participation by all those concerned in the decision making of enterprises and institutions is increasingly being asked for.

It should not be forgotten, though, that a number of authoritarian regimes exist even today, some of them combined with relatively egalitarian economic systems but not with general freedom of expression. The possibility of combining equality with freedom is still questioned by many people.

In recent years the Egalitarian Revolution has reached the field of international relations. Solidarity with the poorer nations has become a political issue in the rich countries and in international organizations. Development aid today represents a tiny fraction of the national incomes of HICs, and it has sometimes been one of the first victims when public expenditures had to be reduced; the important thing to note, however, is that egalitarian ideas do not stop at national frontiers. Nobody knows to what extent solidarity with mankind as a whole will ever become a political reality in the well-to-do societies. Once raised, however, the question of worldwide equality is not likely to be forgotten.

As already mentioned, this brief review of some important steps in the process of innovation is no attempt to write a theory of history. Its purpose has been to serve as a background for the empirical analysis of recent development contained in the following chapters.

To the extent possible this analysis covers the 122 countries listed in Table A.1 in the Annex. They are divided into several groups according to their income levels (GNP per capita). Groups 1 and 2 are described as HICs, Groups 3 through 5 as MICs, and Groups 6 and 7 as LICs.

How are these countries placed in relation to the six revolutions mentioned above? More particularly, how are they placed in relation to what Gordon Childe called "the main stream of human progress?"

Geographically this main stream started with the Agricultural Revolution in West Asia and continued with the Urban Revolution in Mesopotamia and Egypt. Then it moved through ancient Greece and Rome to Western Europe, where the last four Revolutions originated. From there it moved across the oceans to the other continents, which have been influenced by it to varying degrees.

The importance of this main stream should not be overestimated. Independently, important developments in the ways of life and of thinking took place far back in historic and prehistoric time in India, China, Africa, and North and South America. However, those countries that have gradually adopted all the results of the main stream as they developed are in a special position today. Through a long and continuous process they have been able to apply more and more knowledge to all their activities, reaching in this way the level determined by the presently existing knowledge.

The category of HICs consists of 20 countries, all of which either are in Western Europe or have in various ways inherited virtually all the results of the main stream through a relatively continuous process. The United States, Canada, Australia, and New Zealand represent societies that can be considered an outgrowth of Western Europe. East Germany and Czechoslovakia have until recently belonged to larger countries or empires of a Western European type. Puerto Rico owes its high income level to its close links with the U.S. economy, and the society of Israel was created mainly through an inflow of people, capital, and knowledge from Western industrial countries.

The LICs have, with a few exceptions, been European colonies for quite a long period. The main exception is China, which was, however, dependent on European countries and on the United States during the later phase of colonialism.

In the colonial period only small enclaves with European types of activities were established, including some plantations, some mining facilities, and public administration and banking. The large majority of the population was as a rule affected only slightly, and in some cases, at least, the effect was rather harmful. Not only were a large number of persons carried away as slaves, but local handicrafts were sometimes partly destroyed through the competition from European industry, and plantations sometimes expanded at the expense of local food production. In fairness it must be added that a small number of people in these countries got an education and some experience, which have proved useful since independence. Likewise, health services and other institutions were established to make it possible for some infrastructures to be taken over by the new governments at the end of the colonial period.

This is no place for drawing up a balance sheet for colonialism. It must suffice to note that until recently the LICs as a whole have only been touched sporadically by the main stream of innovation described above. They have consequently remained poor, agricultural societies with small and often weak urban sectors.

It follows that most of today's technical and similar knowledge is ill-adapted to these societies. If it is tranferred to them without careful adaptation a large element of discontinuity and disharmony is introduced into their development process.

Between these two extremes lie the MICs. The 52 countries belonging to this category can be grouped as follows:

USSR and Eastern Europe	7
Southern Europe	4
Latin America	20
North and South Africa	4
East Asia	7
Oil-exporting countries	4
Ireland, Lebanon, Jordan, Ivory Coast, Ghana, and Papua and New Guinea	6
Total	52

Eastern Europe, including Russia, was touched much less by the later phases of the "main stream" than were the countries of Western Europe. The same is true of Southern Europe. Spain and Portugal were active in the early stages of the Maritime Revolution and in the colonization of Latin America, but their own societies remained largely feudal and until recently they were only rather slightly touched by the Scientific, Industrial, and Egalitarian Revolutions.

Latin America was colonized by Spain and Portugal. It differs from North America in two respects: firstly, the European element is much smaller than the original Indian population; secondly, this European element seems largely to have kept the traditions and structures of the European countries from which it came. Like Spain and Portugal it has therefore been affected only a little by the later phases of the main stream of Revolutions referred to above.

The same can be said about South Africa and Rhodesia, where the white population of Dutch and British origin seems to have maintained much of the philosophy of European countries, but kept it as it was when their forefathers emigrated. The same probably applies to some extent to the white population of Latin America, and it may be a general feature of small populations that have lived for a long time in a foreign cultural environment.

Two North African countries, Algeria and Tunisia, have for a long time been closely linked to the French community, and they have no doubt received quite a bit of modern knowledge through this connection with a Western European country. Algeria, furthermore, is an oil exporting country.

The other four oil exporting countries are Iran, Iraq, Libya, and Saudi Arabia. They owe much of their economic standard to revenues from the export of oil.

The seven MICs of East Asia are Japan, Hong Kong, North Korea, Taiwan, Malaysia, Singapore, and Mongolia. Japan deliberately started a development based on the application of modern knowledge through the Meiji restoration in 1887-88. Except Mongolia, the other countries mentioned have had a rather lively contact with Western Europe, Japan, and the United States.

Of the last six countries listed above, Ireland has lived more in isolation than most of Western Europe. Lebanon has been a kind of trading center in the West Asian region. The Ivory Coast has been rather closely linked with France, as Papua in New Guinea still is with Australia.

The MICs are a mixed group of countries, and generalizations about them are difficult. Nearly all of them have taken part in the main stream of innovations to a larger extent than the LICs but less so than the HICs. There can hardly be any doubt that participation in this relatively continuous process has been an important factor in determining the placing of countries in the ranking according to income levels shown in Annex Table 1.

Another, equally important, conclusion to be drawn is that as a general rule the techniques and organizational systems of MICs probably are closer to those of the HICs than are those of all the LICs. Less adaptation should therefore be necessary in the further development of these countries. It is hardly necessary to add that each country is an individual case and that in larger countries there can be considerable regional differences within the same national unit.

It remains that the historical inheritance a country has carried with it into the present phase of development will be one of the most important factors determining the problems it will have to deal with in the foreseeable future.

NOTES

1. V. Gordon Childe, *What Happened in History*, rev. ed. (Middlesex, Eng.: Harmondsworth, 1972), Author's Preface.

2. See, among others, Childe, op. cit.; Carlo M. Cipolla, *The Economic History of Population*, rev. ed. (Middlesex, Eng.: Harmondsworth, 1970); and Glyn Daniel, *The First Civilizations*, (Middlesex, Eng.: Harmondsworth, 1971).

3. Cipolla, op. cit., pp. 24-25.

4. Daniel, op. cit., p. 46.

5. Daniel, op. cit., p. 66.

6. Childe, op. cit., p. 290.

4

ECONOMIC DEVELOPMENT

NATURE OF THE PROCESS

As described in Chapter 3, innovation leads to various kinds of structural change in human society. The one effect that most people immediately think of in connection with innovation is increase of production; that is, economic growth. To measure this growth one needs a common unit for all the goods and services produced. If they are measured by their money values we get the gross national product (GNP). It is not necessary here to discuss the imperfection of GNP as an indicator of human welfare, since this in fact is not its purpose. Any description of welfare must take into account a number of factors, as will be discussed in Chapter 5. How these so-called social indicators develop depends, among other things, on the results of production. Therefore the per capita GNP is one of the factors determining what kind of welfare there can be, although by no means the only one. It has, however, been a major objective of the policies of most countries in recent years to obtain a considerable growth of GNP, just as most people want to increase their own incomes as much as they can. This is why economic growth is the first aspect of the development process to be described and analyzed empirically in this book.

Referring to our definition of innovation as the application of more knowledge to human activities, it can be said about the present phase of history that countries differ very much in the degree to which they have applied the existing knowledge.

This being so, the most rapid economic growth should be expected to take place in countries that have reached a stage at which they can begin to apply a great deal more of the existing knowledge. This requires capital for investment. It is through investment in new types of physical capital that much of the most important innovation takes place.

Innovation also requires a considerable amount of knowledge embodied in men, as described in Chapter 2. Only if this condition is fulfilled can new types of machinery and other inventions be constructed and utilized effectively.

It was said in Chapter 2 that capital and knowledge are the two main factors of development. There is an enormous stock of knowledge existing in the world today, but in order to apply the more advanced parts of it countries need capital for investment and a reasonably high standard of education.

As a general rule medium income countries do meet these two requirements to such an extent that they can attain a fairly rapid economic growth. The two other main categories of countries have a slower growth, but for very different reasons. In the case of high income countries it is because they already do apply modern knowledge to a very large extent. As for the low income countries, the reason is that they are too weak, both in capital and knowledge; their progress is therefore rather slow.

This applies to the growth of GNP as such. It also applies to the development of average income levels, which can be measured by the growth of GNP per capita. As a general rule one can say that population growth rates are high in LICs, somewhat lower in MICs, and much lower in HICs. The reasons for these differences will be discussed in Chapter 6. Here it must suffice to note that when we divide the GNP growth rates referred to above by these population growth rates, we find that GNP per capita is growing very fast in MICs, somewhat slower in HICs, but much slower in LICs. In the really poor countries the advance in income levels has usually been modest, and this is so because growth in GNP has been rather slow, while at the same time growth in population has been rapid.

What I have just said represents an important reason for distinguishing between three categories of countries instead of two. It is misleading to talk about developed and developing countries and then to say, as is often done, that the gap between them is widening. In fact the gap between HICs and MICs is narrowing, and, as will be seen in the following section of this chapter, most MICs are developing countries according to the usual terminology. The gap is widening between MICs and LICs; this is both because the latter have a relatively slow economic growth and because their population growth rates are high.

Thus, as a general rule the MICs are catching up with the HICs, while the LICs are lagging behind. This is what one should expect on the basis of the analysis undertaken in this and the previous chapters. In the following section of this chapter it will be shown that recent development is in conformity with this analysis.

It is one of the really great questions regarding development, whether in due course the present LICs will be able to catch up with the two richer categories of countries or whether they will continue to be much poorer during that part of the future about which we can form an opinion. This will be a major subject to be dealt with in Chapter 9.

RECENT ECONOMIC DEVELOPMENT

How does actual development compare with the above description of the process of economic development? An effort to throw some light on this question has been made in Table 4.1, which contains information about the growth of population and GNP of 122 countries, that is, all countries in the world having more than 1 million inhabitants, from 1960 to 1970. They are divided into seven groups according to their income levels (GNP per capita) in 1967, which is the first year for which the relevant information is contained in the Atlas.

The period covered by the table is of course rather short, but it is only from around 1960 that virtually all areas in the world have been organized as sovereign states. Not only has the existing knowledge been at a higher level in recent years than ever before, but for the first time economic development has been an explicit goal for nearly all governments. There are therefore some advantages in concentrating on the recent past.

The most important column in Table 4.1 is the last one, which shows the annual growth of GNP per capita of the population.

As may be expected from the general considerations in the previous section, this growth has been fastest in those groups that are at medium levels of income. If we think of countries as moving upward in levels of GNP per capita—and this is what most countries are doing—then as a rather general rule we can expect growth to be slow during the earlier parts of the process and then faster, since even slow growth creates a basis for further growth. Later on growth will slow down because a stage will have been reached at which the existing knowledge is already utilized to a large extent.

If a poor country begins to develop economically, its progress will usually remain slow for a rather long time. Saving of capital is very small because of the low income level, and most of the population will be illiterate, with very few who are able to teach compared with the large number of those who need to be taught. Furthermore, the results of the educational effort will not influence production much in the first years, especially in general education, where children and adolescents may have to go to school many years before entering the labor force. Also, the investment in infrastructure will show its results only over a long period, especially in a newly independent country, for which a government machinery has to be set up and some practical experience must be gained before it can function smoothly.

After this slow process has gone on for some years it may gradually gather momentum. Even a modest development creates some of the conditions for further development. Some experience is gained; the standard of education improves somewhat; and savings can be increased. The country will progressively become better equipped to absorb foreign aid and private investment by firms from richer countries. Also, its own accumulation of capital will increase.

The highest rate of economic development is usually attained when a country has advanced so much that modern techniques can begin to spread quickly, while at the same time people move on a large scale from agriculture into industry and services, which can now absorb them. Agriculture will then become more mechanized, enabling production per man in the farm sector to catch up with the production of other sectors.

When this rapid expansion has continued for some time, development will usually begin to slow down somewhat. Modern techniques will now have been applied in large parts of the economy, and there will therefore be less to be

TABLE 4.1

Growth of Population and GNP, 1960-70

Group	Number of Countries	GNP per Capita 1967 (dollars)	Population 1967 (millions)	GNP 1967 (billions of dollars)	Average GNP per Capita 1967 (dollars)	Annual Growth, 1960-70 (percent)		
						Population	GNP	GNP per capita
1	9	1,801 or more	306.6	955.5	3,120	1.2	4.6	3.4
2	11	1,101-1,800	238.4	354.3	1,490	0.8	4.3	3.5
3	11	701-1,100	443.8	413.9	930	1.2	7.8	6.5
4	15	401- 700	160.9	89.2	550	2.2	6.7	4.4
5	26	201- 400	299.3	80.0	270	2.9	5.9	2.9
6	26	101- 200	375.6	50.4	130	2.5	5.2	2.6
7	24	100 or less	1,580.4	138.6	90	2.2	3.9	1.7
Total	122		3,405.0	2,081.9	610	2.0	5.3	3.2

Note: A list of these countries indicating the size of their population and GNP per capita is given in Annex Table A.1.

Source: World Bank Atlas 1969 and 1972 (Washington, D.C.: International Bank for Reconstruction and Development), first two tables.

gained from further modernization. At the same time the agricultural population will have been reduced to such an extent that it no longer represents a
reserve of industrial manpower of any importance. In the United Kingdom, the
oldest industrial country, agriculture now employs only about 3 percent of the
population.

How far development can proceed depends on the level of what I have
called "the existing knowledge," more than on anything else. If this level were
constant over a long period, more and more of this existing knowledge would
become embodied in men and in capital, and production per capita would then
gradually approach a ceiling determined by the level of existing knowledge. The
total process of development from the slow beginning until this advanced stage
of near-stagnation would then have followed a course of the type indicated by
"curve a" in Figure 4.1. There would be a turning point (t_a) at which the rate
of development would begin to slow down.

In a period in which knowledge is expanding rapidly, as at present, the
process will be somewhat different. Development will be faster at all levels, but
particularly in the more developed countries, at least at the beginning, because
most of the new knowledge will be produced in these countries and therefore
adapted to their situation. The ceiling determined by the existing knowledge
will not be constant, but will be moving upwards and therefore not acting as a
ceiling as long as new knowledge is produced. We then get a development of the
type indicated by "curve b" in Figure 4.1. The turning point (t_b) will under

FIGURE 4.1

Growth of GNP per Capita

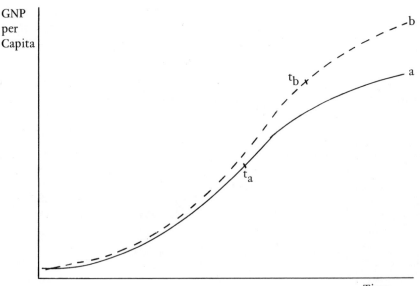

these circumstances be reached at a more advanced stage of development than in the first case.

If the increase in the existing knowledge goes on for a long time, more and more knowledge will be transferred to the economically less developed countries and adapted to their situation. They may then begin to catch up with the more developed societies. In that case the turning point will again move somewhat to the left. The possibilities of such a development will be discussed in Chapter 9.

Thus, if there is something that can be called the typical growth curve for GNP per capita, it is not an exponential curve but rather an S-shaped curve that may or may not approach an upper limit. This of course means that there are no sharp division-lines between the fast-growing MICs in the middle of the curve and the two slow-growing categories at its lower and upper ends. It is a matter of judgment where to place the limits of the three categories.

It is obvious from Table 4.1 that Groups 1 and 2 can be characterized as HICs; Groups 3 and 4 as MICs; and Groups 6 and 7 as LICs.

The GNP growth of Group 5 is fairly rapid, but because it has the highest population growth rate of all the groups its GNP per capita has not been growing very fast. There are, however, signs of a speeding up of this growth. As can be seen from Table 4.3, growth has been much faster in the period 1968-72 than in 1961-67 for those regions in which most of the countries of Group 5 lie, and there are two reasons for this. One is that these countries have now reached a stage at which they are able to apply new knowledge on a larger scale; the other is that their labor force is now growing faster than in the 1960s. Because of the rapid population growth a particularly large percentage of the population of Group 5 countries was below 15 years of age. These adolescents and children are now becoming adults and entering the labor force.

In the tables that follow, MICs will therefore be defined as comprising Groups 3, 4, and 5 on Table 4.1. It is possible to combine the distinction between the three main categories of countries with the regional comparisons that are made in much of the literature about development by excluding four of the 122 countries dealt with in Table 4.1. These four countries are Puerto Rico, Israel, Bolivia, and Haiti. Further explanation is given in the Annex.

In Table 4.2, economic development for the main categories and regions during the 1960s is described in the same way it was described for the seven groups in Table 4.1. The first region in the table is composed of four countries: the United States, Canada, Australia, and New Zealand. All of them belong to Group 1. Because of their fast population growth Group 1 as a whole has a higher population growth rate than Group 2. (See Table 4.1.)

Among the MICs the countries of Latin America are showing remarkably high rates of population growth, with the exception of Argentina, Uruguay, and Jamaica. This general feature of the Latin American region will be discussed further in Chapter 6. It is one of the reasons why GNP per capita has been growing so slowly in Latin America. However, GNP as such has also been growing more slowly in most Latin American countries than in other MICs. A speeding up has taken place in recent years, however, as seen in Table 4.3.

The high growth rates of Japan are well known. For its reconstruction after World War II Japan imported modern technology on a large scale. It

TABLE 4.2

Growth of Population and GNP, by Categories and Regions, 1960-70

	Number of Countries	Population 1967 (millions)	GNP 1967 (billions of dollars)	GNP per Capita 1967 (dollars)	Annual Growth, 1960-70 (percent)		
					Population	GNP	GNP per capita
HICs	18	539.6	1,303.3	2,420	1.0	4.5	3.5
North America and Oceania	4	234.1	807.8	3,450	1.3	4.5	3.2
Europe	14	305.5	495.5	1,620	0.8	4.5	3.7
MICs	52	904.0	583.1	650	1.9	7.4	5.4
Japan	1	99.9	99.9	1,000	1.0	10.7	9.6
USSR	1	235.5	228.4	970	1.2	7.1	5.8
Latin America	20	245.1	98.6	400	2.9	5.3	2.3
Other MICs	30	323.5	156.2	480	1.9	7.1	5.1
LICs	48	1,947.6	188.1	100	2.3	4.3	2.0
Asia	18	1,680.6	160.1	100	2.2	4.3	2.1
Africa	30	267.0	28.0	100	2.6	4.4	1.8
Total	118	3,391.2	2,074.5	610	2.0	5.3	3.2

Source: *World Bank Atlas 1969* and *1972* (Washington, D.C.: International Bank for Reconstruction and Development).

could be applied because the standard of education was high as the result of a deliberate policy since the Meiji restoration.

It is worth noting that a few other countries in East Asia, namely, Hong Kong, South Korea, and Taiwan, have had growth rates almost equal to that of Japan. All three of these countries have had rather close ties with the Japanese economy, and the two latter also with the United States.

Comments on the USSR will be made below, as part of a general discussion of economic development in socialist countries.

The subgroup "Other MICs" includes countries in various parts of the world, as can be seen from the general survey of MICs in Chapter 3. It is therefore not surprising that its average growth rates are close to those of MICs as a whole.

Most of the countries in Asia and Africa belong to the category of LICs. Apart from Israel, which is not included i this table, the total population of the countries on these two continents is distributed as follows:

	Asia (millions)	Africa (millions)
MICs	221.7	53.0
LICs	1,680.6	267.0
Total	1,902.3	320.0

The Asian MICs are Japan, Iran, Turkey, and some smaller countries in East and West Asia. In Africa the MICs are mainly found in the northern and southern parts of the continent (Algeria, Tunisia, South Africa, and Rhodesia). As a general rule it can therefore be said that the category of LICs includes South and Southeast Asia, China, and tropical Africa. It will be seen from the table that GNP has been growing at virtually the same speed on each continent. Mainly because of China, the total of Asian LICs has a lower average population growth rate than that of African LICs, and consequently a slightly faster growth of GNP per capita.

It will be of interest to add a few remarks about socialist countries as compared with other countries. By socialist countries, I shall understand only those usually described as such in international statistics; that is, the USSR, the countries of Eastern Europe, Cuba, China, Mongolia, North Korea, and North Vietnam.

There are no socialist countries in Group 1. Concerning the other groups in Table 4.1, the average annual growth of GNP from 1960 to 1970 was as follows:

Group	Socialist Countries (percent)	Other Countries (percent)
2	4.0	2.8
3	5.9	7.9
4	5.2	4.2
5	2.7	3.0
6	3.2	2.6
7	2.1	1.3

TABLE 4.3

Growth of Population and GDP, 1950-72, in Percent per Year[a]

	Population			GNP[b]			GNP per capita		
	1950-60	1961-67	1968-72	1950-60	1961-67	1968-72	1950-60	1961-67	1969-72
Industrialized Countries	1.2	1.2	1.0	4.0	5.1	4.5	2.8	3.8	3.5
Developing Countries	2.2	2.4	2.4	4.6	5.2	6.2	2.3	2.7	3.7
Southern Europe	1.4	1.5	1.5	5.2	6.9	6.8	3.7	5.3	5.2
Latin America	2.8	2.9	2.9	5.0	5.1	6.4	2.1	2.1	3.4
Middle East	3.0	3.0	3.0	6.0	7.2	9.2	2.9	4.1	6.1
East Asia	2.5	2.5	2.5	4.7	6.0	7.4	2.1	3.4	4.8
South Asia	1.9	2.4	2.3	3.6	3.7	3.7	1.7	1.4	1.4
Africa	2.3	2.5	2.6	4.0	3.9	5.8	1.7	1.4	2.1

aThe socialist countries are not included.

bFor 1950-60 the growth rates relate to GDP (Gross Domestic Product). The difference between these and GNP growth rates should be neglegible, since GDP is equal to GNP less net earnings of interest from abroad.

Sources: Lester B. Pearson, *Partners in Development* (New York, Praeger Publishers 1969), p. 358; and World Bank/IDA, *Annual Report* Washington, D.C. 1973), Table 1.

It will be seen that there is no systematic difference between the two types of countries. Group 3 is dominated by the USSR and Japan, where the latter has had the highest growth rate. Similarly, Group 7 is dominated by China and India, where the former has had the fastest growth. The other four groups taken together represent less than 10 percent of the total population of socialist countries. There is therefore no general indication that in recent years socialist countries have had either a faster or a slower economic development than other countries.

One final remark can be made concerning the information contained in Table 4.2. It is remarkable that in all three main categories of countries the growth rates for GNP vary much less than those for GNP per capita. This means that, other things being equal, countries with a relatively slow population growth seem to have had a faster growth of GNP per capita than those having a faster population growth. This applies to Europe as compared with North America and Oceania; to Japan and the USSR as compared with Latin America and other MICs; and to Asia as compared with Africa.

In explanation of this fact, it can be assumed that population growth gives a rough indication of the growth of one factor of production, namely labor. However, economic development also depends on the growth of capital and knowledge. It is more difficult to raise the general level of capital and knowledge where much of the effort made is needed simply to keep step with a fast population growth, than where this is not so.

This is, of course, particularly important if one considers a longer period than a single decade. In that case it is also to be remembered that the quantity of land, on the whole, is constant. As a rule the quantity of land per capita is decreasing, therefore, and the more population increases, the more important is this decrease. I shall come back to these aspects of development in Chapter 9.

LONGER-TERM TRENDS

As mentioned earlier, it is only from about 1960 that virtually all countries have been sovereign states pursuing deliberate development policies. It would nevertheless be of interest to look at a somewhat longer period. The information available for the 1950s and for the period since 1970 is less complete than that for the 1960s, but it does make our picture of recent development more complete.

In Table 4.3, "Industrialized Countries" roughly speaking corresponds to Groups 1-3 in Table 4.1. The first four "Developing Countries" represent the countries of Groups 4 and 5 in general, while South Asia and Africa can be taken as representing Groups 6 and 7, China not included.

It could be expected that economic growth would be faster after 1960 than earlier, since deliberate efforts to further such growth became widespread about that time.

It has sometimes been assumed that rapid economic growth in the rich countries is an important condition for a similar development of the poor ones, since it creates an expanding market for their raw materials and other primary products. It is therefore interesting to see from Table 4.3 that growth became faster in most groups of "developing countries" in 1968-72, although at the same time it became slower in the industrialized countries. This may raise doubts about the contention sometimes heard, that the industrial countries can help the developing countries more by expanding rapidly themselves than by anything else. In fact it would be more reasonable to infer from Table 4.3 that, in general, development efforts are beginning to bear fruit.

The slight reduction in the growth rate of Southern Europe for the period 1968-72 can perhaps be explained by the fact that the economy of this region is particularly closely linked to that of Northern Europe, from which it gets revenue from exports, tourism, and migrant workers.

As regards South Asia, the lack of progress in 1968-72 compared with 1961-67 is due to bad harvests in 1971, when agricultural production was reduced by .1 percent, and even more in 1972, when it dropped by no less than 5.6 percent. For 1968-70 the average annual growth of GNP was 5 percent.

From the considerations above it would appear that there has been no close correlation between the economic growth of the industrialized countries and that of "developing countries." There has probably not been any clear relationship between the volume of development assistance and the economic development of the aid-receiving countries, either. According to OECD statistics[1] the net flow of official development assistance from the 16 members of OECD's Development Assistance Committee (DAC) has been as follows (in billions of dollars counted at the 1970 price level):

	Assistance (billions of dollars at 1970 price level)	Grants and Grant-like Elements (percent)
1961	6.2	77
1967	7.1	55
1972	7.3	51

Thus there has been no substantial increase in development assistance in the period 1968-72, while the economic growth of the developing countries has speeded up. It should be noted that these figures include the contributions of DAC countries to multilateral agencies.

It can be added that technical assistance represented 15 percent of the aid flow in 1961, 20 percent in 1967, and 21 percent in 1972. This means that the transfer of knowledge has increased somewhat faster than the transfer of capital. In fact, the relative importance of technical assistance is greater than these figures would lead one to believe, since in contrast to loans it does not result in any burden in the form of interest and repayment of debt.

It would accord with the general reasoning of this book if increased importance were attached to technical assistance in aid programs. Not only is knowledge the leading factor of development, but also the gap between rich and poor countries is even wider in the field of know-how than in the supply of capital. Furthermore, it can be expected that private capital will be attracted by the very fact that economic growth is becoming faster in many MICs and

LICs, as these countries begin to represent markets of some importance and at least part of their labor force becomes increasingly qualified for a number of tasks.

That private capital has actually been flowing to developing countries in larger amounts recently than in earlier years can be seen from the OECD statistics given above. The total flow of private capital measured in the same way as the flow of official aid was as follows:

1961	$3.8 billion
1967	$4.8 billion
1972	$7.3 billion

Thus the private capital flow has been speeding up at the same time as economic development, in the countries that are usually called "developing."

The main conclusions to be drawn from the analysis in the present chapter can be summarized in the following way.

MICs have experienced a faster economic development than both HICs and LICs. This is because as a general rule MICs have reached a stage where they can begin to use modern technical and other knowledge on a larger scale. HICs have already done so, and therefore further advance requires a more specific effort than simply the application of knowledge already at hand. LICs, finally, are still too weak to make more than relatively slow progress. Furthermore, modern knowledge is to a large extent ill-adapted to the circumstances of LICs. Even so, growth of GNP as such has been nearly as fast in these countries as in the HICs, as seen in Table 4.2. Because of rapid population growth, their advance in GNP per capita has been considerably slower than that of the rich countries.

In recent years economic growth has become faster in both MICs and LICs, exception being made for years with bad climatic conditions in some countries. This has happened in spite of the fact that markets in the HICs have been growing more slowly in these years. Also, the flow of aid from the rich countries has been growing very slowly in the last five-year period. It would appear, then, that as far as economic development is concerned, both MICs and LICs have become somewhat less dependent on the evolution and the policies of the rich countries.

Hard and fast conclusions are dangerous, but it does not seem unreasonable to suppose that after some years of independence and deliberate development efforts, many of these countries have gained so much knowledge about appropriate policies that on the whole achievement has improved. The increasing inflow of private capital can probably be taken as a sign of more confidence than before in the economies of a number of these countries.

In conclusion it is appropriate to refer once more to what was said in the introductory remarks of this chapter, namely that GNP per capita is not by itself an indicator of human welfare. It can be used as a measure, though somewhat imperfect, of the total flow of goods and services resulting from a country's productive activities, but what that means in terms of welfare depends on the way in which it is distributed, on the nature of the public services made available, and various other factors.

In order to evaluate the conditions of life of the population one must therefore look at such social indicators as income distribution, nutrition, health, etc. This will be the subject of Chapter 5, one of the purposes of which is to study the relations between social development and the economic development that has been dealt with in this chapter.

NOTE

1. OECD, *Development Cooperation* (Paris: OECD, 1972 and 1973), 1972 Review Table II-1, 1973 Review Table II-2, and Annex II, Table A.

5

SOCIAL DEVELOPMENT

DIFFERENTIATION

The effect of economic development on the conditions of life in a society depends on a number of factors, such as the distribution of the results of production, the organization of health services, and education and other joint activities. In general the advance of knowledge leads to a continuous change in the conditions of human existence and in ways of life. It is the purpose of the present chapter to examine some of these changes as they are described by the so-called social indicators.

Probably none of these changes is more important then the ongoing differentiation of human societies that results from the process of innovation.

In a society dominated by subsistence agriculture, the individual families have approximately the same pattern of activities and probably also approximately the same standard of living. Differentiation begins when it is realized that certain people in a village are more proficient than the others in certain activities. Gradually such persons become specialists in their particular fields and as such the first artisans, such as smiths or weavers.

This specialization makes two important changes in the structure of society: because of it some people have a different kind of life from the others; and also the exchange of goods between artisans and farmers becomes part of the fabric of the village society.

In this way more and more activities are detached from that of farming. Furthermore, entirely new activities come into being, and gradually society becomes more and more differentiated. Agriculture then ceases to be subsistence farming; modern agriculture works primarily for the market.

In Table 5.1 a description is given of the state of differentiation reached in 1960, for 82 of the 122 countries listed in Annex Table A.1. As one of the three sectors generally used in statistical records, agriculture includes horticulture, forestry, keeping of fisheries, and similar primary production.

TABLE 5.1

Distribution of Labor Force by Type of Activity, 1960

Group	Number of Countries	Population 1967 (millions)	Agriculture (percent)	Industry (percent)	Services (percent)
1	9	306.6	10.3	35.3	54.4
2	9	208.7	16.0	44.1	39.9
3	10	208.3	36.5	27.6	35.9
4	13	157.2	45.3	23.4	31.3
5	22	283.5	55.2	15.6	29.2
6	13	260.3	73.7	8.4	17.9
7	6	670.0	73.8	10.7	15.5
Total	82	2,094.6	48.4	21.7	29.2

Source: *ILO Yearbook of Labor Statistics 1970* (Geneva: International Labour Organization).

It is interesting to note how closely this aspect of social development is related to the economic development described in Chapter 4. If we move upwards from the lowest to the highest of the seven income groups, we find that the percentage of the labor force employed in agriculture goes down and that the percentage employed in services goes up, in a rather regular way. The employment in industry reaches its highest level in Group 2. In the rich countries employment is increasing particularly fast in services, partly because industry is being mechanized, but also because activities like transportation, banking, education, and public administration are expanding rapidly. Some of these branches of the service sector are not easily mechanized to the same extent as is industry.

The figures for Group 7 in Table 5.1 are to some extent misleading, since it has only been possible to cover a relatively small proportion of the large population in the poorest countries. If all the countries in Group 7 had been represented in the table the world total would have shown a substantially higher percentage for agriculture.

It would be of interest to study the development of differentiation in all of the countries through the decade 1960-70, as it was done in the last chapter concerning their economic development. Unfortunately it is only possible to do this for a rather small number of countries, as seen in Table 5.2.

On the whole this table seems to confirm the general impression that if we move upwards through the seven income groupings of countries at a certain point of time, we get a picture that illustrates the evolution of the individual countries through a period of time. This is important for the whole analysis undertaken in this book, since only to a limited extent does the existing information permit us to follow a number of countries through a period long enough to be interesting. It is therefore of interest that, concerning a number of aspects of development,

TABLE 5.2

Changes in Distribution of Labor Force by Type of Activity, 1960 and 1970

Group	Number of Countries	Population 1967 (millions)	Agriculture (percent) 1960	Agriculture (percent) 1970	Industry (percent) 1960	Industry (percent) 1970	Services (percent) 1960	Services (percent) 1970
1	4	274.2	9.9	7.1	34.5	33.7	55.6	59.2
2	4	136.2	20.9	20.0	42.6	36.9	36.5	43.1
3	3	119.5	27.2	20.6	31.4	34.3	41.1	45.1
4	2	41.2	41.1	28.8	28.4	35.3	30.5	35.9
5	2	25.8	58.1	47.9	15.2	15.7	26.7	36.4
6	3	174.6	68.9	63.9	9.7	10.2	21.4	25.9
7	—	—	—	—	—	—	—	—
Total	18	771.5	29.1	24.7	30.0	29.7	40.9	45.6

Source: ILO Yearbook of Labor Statistics 1970 and 1972 (Geneva: International Labour Organization).

groups of countries representing various levels of income also represent stages in an ongoing process. More examples of this will be given in what follows.

A comparison of the two tables seems to indicate that differentiation proceeds particularly fast in the medium income countries, which also show the fastest economic growth. Agriculture represents about 71 percent of the total employment in Group 6, but only 16 percent in Group 2. It was to be expected that the same stages in the development process would represent rapid change in a number of fields. It could be added that in fact differentiation is an important factor leading to economic growth because it moves people to sectors with a higher productivity level.

It can perhaps be inferred from Tables 5.1 and 5.2 that the relative decline in employment in industry taking place in high income countries is not likely to lead to a drastic reduction, as has happened in agriculture. Concerning industrial employment, Group 2 seems to approach the lower level of Group 1, which itself does not change very much.

It will also be of interest to study various social indicators as they appear in the major regions of the world, as was done in Chapter 4 concerning economic development. This is done in Table 5.3, which is arranged in the same way as Table 4.2. There are a few figures in this table that can contribute to that fuller and broader understanding of the development process that I hope to further by this book.

In Chapter 4 it was shown that North America and Oceania have a substantially higher income level than Europe. Here we see that these "emigrant societies of European stock" are also more advanced than the old continent in the direction of being service societies.

Another interesting difference is that between Latin America and "Other MICs". They have nearly the same income level, but although the movement

TABLE 5.3

Distribution of Labor Force by Type of Activity, by Categories and Regions, 1960

	Number of Countries	Population 1967 (millions)	Agriculture (percent)	Industry (percent)	Services (percent)
HICs	16	509.9	13.0	38.8	48.2
North America and Oceania	4	234.1	8.3	34.1	57.6
Europe	12	275.8	16.4	42.1	41.5
MICs	45	649.0	45.2	22.5	32.3
Japan	1	99.9	25.3	32.2	42.5
USSR	—	—	—	—	—
Latin America	20	245.1	44.3	19.5	36.2
Other MICs	24	304.0	54.2	20.2	25.6
LICs	17	921.9	73.3	9.9	16.8
Asia	8	856.5	73.1	10.2	16.7
Africa	9	65.4	75.7	6.3	18.0
Total	78	2,080.8	48.3	21.6	30.1

Source: ILO Yearbook of Labor Statistics 1970 (Geneva: International Labour Organization).

out of agriculture has proceeded further in Latin America than in the other group of countries, industrial employment is at a slightly lower level; instead, more people have gone into services. One would expect a broader industrial development when so many people have left agriculture.

There is a similar difference between Asia and Africa in the category of low income countries. Here it is Asia that has a broader industrial base than Africa.

This is the first of a number of cases to be mentioned in this book in which there is an interesting similarity between Africa and Latin America. In the next section it will be shown that these two regions are more likely to have "dual societies" than are Asia and "Other MICs." The modern sector, to which industry belongs, is more of a narrow, isolated enclave in Africa and Latin America than in the two other regions, and some of the troubles of these countries have to do with this lack of integration.

Increasingly industry and services have been concentrated in towns and cities. An important aspect of the process of differentiation is therefore the concentration of more and more people in urban areas, as shown in Table 5.4.

TABLE 5.4

Urbanization

Group	Number of Countries	Population 1967 (millions)	Urban Population (percent) 1960	1970
1	7	236.3	68.9	72.6
2	7	102.2	72.8	73.8
3	7	407.2	52.0	59.3
4	5	76.5	47.2	55.0
5	10	195.7	41.7	50.6
6	7	122.3	30.7	36.8
7	2	631.1	17.0	18.6
Total	45	1,771.3	40.9	44.6

Source: UN Demographic Yearbook 1970 and *1971* (New York: United Nations).

As could be expected, urbanization has proceeded faster in MICs than at the two extremes of the income scale. It is interesting to see, however, that it seems to gather momentum as early as the stage represented by Group 6, although too much should not be concluded from the figures for that group, since they cover only seven countries. They do nevertheless present a picture that is in conformity with the well-known fact that rural-urban migration is proceeding at a disturbing speed in many LICs. This of course is the result of the higher incomes in the modern, urban sector, in comparison with those of the traditional sectors in the rural districts. Further comments on this important problem will be made in the following section of this chapter.

Urbanization takes place because there are advantages to be expected for those who move to the towns and cities. It also has a number of advantages for society as a whole, enabling enterprises to become bigger and creating big enough markets for specialized activities. There are, however, also disadvantages when urban agglomerations become very big and very crowded. It is therefore interesting to note that according to Table 5.3 urbanization is now proceeding rather slowly in the HICs; it may well be that we are approaching an upper limit in this respect. More will be said about this in Chapter 9.

INCOME DISTRIBUTION

Differentiation means the tendency of members of a society to live increasingly under circumstances that vary from those of other members in various respects. Of particular importance from a social point of view is the question of whether the distribution of income varies in any regular way during the development process.

Theoretical considerations would lead one to believe that there will normally be some regularity in the evolution of income distribution. People move from agriculture to other activities mainly because they can earn more in this way. In a more general way one would expect people to move toward those sectors where they get the best reward for their work. The fast-expanding sectors must therefore offer particularly high incomes in order to attract enough people. We are here faced with what we might call "sectoral inequality of incomes."

There are other inequalities. Within each sector some enterprises gradually become bigger than others; this development has no doubt been favored by the process of differentiation, and even started by that process. In subsistence agriculture farms are likely to have a size that corresponds to the needs and the working capacity of the type of family that is usual in the society in question. When farmers begin to sell part of their produce, those with large farms can obtain higher incomes than those with small ones. Similar differences have gradually come into being in industry and in many branches of the service sector.

A very important aspect of the inequality thus arising is that it is not only a difference in levels of income, but also a difference in social status. In the traditional village the big farmer is a more important person than the small peasant, and in many national societies the landowning aristocracy has been a politically dominant class through long historical periods.

There is another difference that results from the increase in size of enterprises, in the other sectors as well as in agriculture. This is the difference in status between the owner-manager and his subordinates. Big enterprises will have a pyramidal structure, with the managing director at the top and the unskilled workers at the bottom. In this case, too, a difference in status and a difference in income level will usually go together. This means that alongside of sectoral inequality of incomes there has developed something that might be called "hierarchical inequality," accompanied by an inequality in social status.

Last comes the "geographical inequality" of incomes that is so important in the world today. There are differences in income levels among countries, as described in Chapter 4, but regional differences can also be substantial within an individual country. Brazil and Italy are typical examples of countries in which this is the case.

There are in particular two reasons why geographical inequality has become so important. One is that some countries have been longer and more continuously than others in "the main stream of progress" described by Gordon Childe. (See Chapter 3 of this book.) This is the main reason for the differences between the three categories HICs, MICs, and LICs. The other reason, of course, is that some countries or regions are particularly richly endowed with natural resources.

Of the three kinds of inequality mentioned, it is obvious that sectoral inequality has generally been particularly important between the agricultural and nonagricultural sectors, since this difference in earnings has been the main factor inducing people to move out of agriculture. It follows that there is less need for such inequality when the exodus from agriculture is drawing toward its close, as it seems to be in many HICs. In fact, in HICs incomes in agriculture tend to catch up with those of the other sectors, which is necessary to prevent an outflow that goes too far.

Also, hierarchical inequality has usually been reduced after a certain point in the development of countries that have been continuously in the main stream of progress. The investment of more and more capital per worker, as well as the increasing level of technical and other knowledge, are factors that bring about a steady increase in the productivity of labor and therefore higher levels of real income for workers. At the same time, financial techniques such as those of the corporation and the banking system make it possible to spread the ownership of the capital invested in agriculture and industry much more widely than it is spread at the earlier stage at which the dominating people are the big landowners and the first "captains of industry." From that stage onwards, inequality of incomes will therefore usually decrease.

It would be well to test these theoretical considerations by means of an empirical examination of income distribution as it actually exists in countries of various types. Unfortunately, information is rather scarce on this important subject, and it is not easy to measure the inequality of income distribution in a simple and unequivocal way.

An instrument used for the description of income distribution is the so-called Lorenz curve.[1] An example of such a curve is shown in Figure 5.1. Cumulative percentages of income recipients are shown along the horizontal axis, and cumulative percentages of income along the vertical axis. Beginning with the lowest incomes and ending with the highest ones, we get a curve the shape of which describes the income distribution of the society in question.

If distribution were absolutely equal, the first 10 percent of the population would have 10 percent of the total income of the country, and so on. The Lorenz curve would then follow the straight line OB. The more it deviates from that line, the more unequal is the distribution of income.

A measure of this inequality is the so-called Gini ratio, which is the ratio between the area A and the area of the whole triangle OBC. It follows that the Gini ratio can vary between O and I. It will be O with absolute equality of income distribution.

There can, however, be a number of different Lorenz curves representing the same Gini ratio. In Figure 5.2 an alternative example is shown. Like the curve in Figure 5.1 it represents a Gini ratio of .5, but the two curves describe the income structure of societies that are very different.

Figure 5.1 describes the situation of a country in which there is a gradual transition from the lowest incomes to the highest ones, so that all income levels in between are represented in a fairly even way. This will usually be the case in countries that have gone through a rather long and continuous development. In these countries differentiation has proceeded in a progressive way, whereby both an upper class and various types of middle class groups have come into being. Such an income structure can therefore be expected in most HICs and MICs, as well as in those LICs that have been in the "main stream of progress" discussed in Chapter 3 for a reasonably long time, but which are poor because they are poorly endowed with natural resources.

A different type of income structure is shown in Figure 5.2, which illustrates an extreme case of what is now often called a "dual economy" or

FIGURE 5.1

Income Distribution Curve

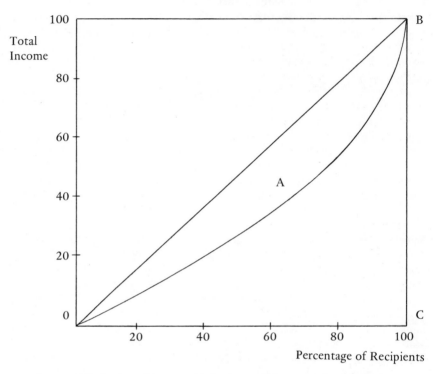

Source: Felix Paukert, "Income Distribution at Different Levels of Development: A Survey of Evidence," *International Labour Review* 108, nos. 2 and 3, pp. 97-125.

"dual society." By this term is meant a poor country in which there is a small modern sector with much higher incomes than are obtained in the large traditional sector.

This dualism is one of the major problems of development today. It arises through the transfer of technology from HICs with little or no adaptation. The modern sector comprises industry, wholesale trade, banks, plantations, mining, a few universities, and part of the public administration. Those working in this sector can not only obtain higher incomes than people in the traditional sector, but also have a higher social status. Since many of them have a European type of education they will also often represent an enclave in the cultural pattern of the country.

Their isolation from the majority of the people is reinforced by the fact that the modern sector or at least its management is concentrated in the few large cities. The big enterprises will often be linked more closely to the foreign corporations of which they are subsidiaries than to the main part of the economy of their host country.

FIGURE 5.2

Income Distribution Curve in a Dual Society

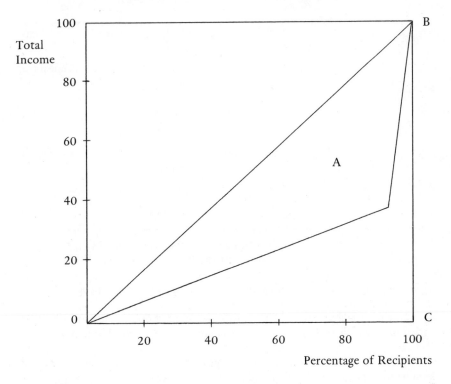

Source: Felix Paukert, "Income Distribution at Different Levels of Development: A Survey of Evidence," *International Labour Review* 108, nos. 2 and 3, pp. 97-125.

As already mentioned, Figure 5.2 illustrates an extreme case of such a dual society, since the modern sector represents only 10 percent of the total population, but 60 percent of the total income of the country. In most cases the division-line is less sharp; there are usually some small-scale industries and medium-sized farms, and also a number of employees and skilled workers with reasonably good incomes. Figures 5.1 and 5.2 therefore illustrate two clearly distinct variants. Most countries may be placed somewhere in between.

The article by Felix Paukert from which Figures 5.1 and 5.2 are taken contains information about the Gini ratio for 52 countries at various income levels. In Table 5.5 they are grouped in seven groups, in the same way as in Table 4.1.

As could be expected, the highest Gini ratios are found at about the middle of the income scale. This seems to confirm the hypothesis that in the earlier phases of the process of differentiation inequality of incomes increases. The new and expanding sectors have the highest income levels, while

TABLE 5.5

Income Distribution

Group	Number of Countries	Population 1967 (millions)	Gini Ratio
1	6	277.3	.37
2	7	190.1	.41
3	5	142.3	.40
4	7	81.4	.53
5	9	153.1	.54
6	9	110.5	.46
7	9	754.4	.36
Total	52	1,709.1	.40

Source: Felix Paukert, "Income Distribution at Different Levels of Development: A Survey of Evidence," *International Labour Review* 108, nos. 2 and 3, pp. 97-125.

agriculture lags behind. This difference in earnings encourages people to move out of agriculture into the expanding sectors.

During the later stages of the process a labor shortage begins to be felt in agriculture, which is then forced to mechanize. Thereby productivity is raised, and agriculture begins to catch up with the other sectors.

What has just been said about agriculture will usually also apply to handicrafts and to small-scale retail trade. This is why in a general way income distribution is again becoming more equal in the later phases of the process of differentiation.

In Table 5.6 the same analysis is undertaken with countries arranged according to the categories and regions to which they belong.

It is in conformity with the theoretical considerations outlined above that inequality of incomes is particularly pronounced in MICs, while there is more equality in both LICs and HICs. That Japan has a relatively low Gini ratio is understandable because it is on the verge of being an HIC.

As regards LICs, it is a striking fact that the Gini ratio is much higher for Africa than for Asia. This can partly be explained by the fact that the low figure for Asia is strongly influenced by that for India, which is only .33. Unfortunately, the figures for the individual countries refer to years that differ rather greatly from one country to another. For most countries they refer to some years in the decade 1960-70, but for India they refer to 1956-57. There can hardly be any doubt that since then inequality has increased in India in an important way. As will be shown in a later section, the nutritional standard was lower in 1970 than in 1960, in spite of the fact that GNP per capita had increased by 1.1 percent per year during the decade. It seems likely, therefore, that this increase has to a large extent benefited the wealthier part of the

TABLE 5.6

Income Distribution, by Categories and Regions

	Number of Countries	Population 1967 (millions)	Gini Ratio
HICs	11	462.0	0.39
North America and Oceania	2	210.9	0.34
Europe	9	251.1	0.43
MICs	21	376.8	0.48
Japan	1	99.9	0.39
USSR	—	—	—
Latin America	13	219.3	0.52
Other MICs	7	57.6	0.50
LICs	17	861.1	0.37
Asia	6	733.1	0.34
Africa	11	128.0	0.52
Total	49	1,699.9	0.39

Source: Felix Paukert, "Income Distribution at Different Levels of Development: A Survey of Evidence," *International Labour Review* 108, nos. 2 and 3, pp. 97-125.

population, while the living standard of the poorer part deteriorated. This impression is strengthened by the well-known fact that the Green Revolution, with its introduction of especially high-yielding varieties of wheat to India, has been to the advantage of the bigger farmers more than the smaller ones. It has also furthered mechanization on the bigger farms and thereby reduced the demand for the work of landless laborers. Since India represents 511.1 million out of the 733.1 million total population of the six Asian LICs in the table, a later and more realistic figure for that country probably would have raised the figure for Asia in an important way.

It remains, however, that most of the African countries have substantially higher figures than most of the Asian countries. This seems to indicate a difference between the two continents in the nature of their development process.

Firm conclusions cannot, of course, be drawn from information about a limited number of countries. It is, nevertheless, interesting to note that the impression one gets from the figures is confirmed by a look at the historical development.

There can be no doubt that on the whole Asia has been in the "main stream of progress" for a longer period and in a more continuous way than

Africa. It follows that as a general rule the income structure of Asian countries would be closer to the pattern shown in Figure 5.1 than that of African countries, which would be more similar to that of Figure 5.2. The modern sector is therefore on the whole more integrated in a network of older, small- and medium sized enterprises in Asia than it is in Africa, and there has been more time to develop agriculture, using, for example, draught animals in the cultivation of rice. Thus the longer and more continuous process of innovation in Asia has brought about income structures that are less marked by the features of a dual society than those of Africa.

In the analysis undertaken above it has not been possible to include information about any of the socialist countries. Presumably income distribution is relatively equal in those countries, since earnings from land and capital belong to the community as such as a matter of principle. Private plots for the farming population do exist, however, both in the USSR and in China, and incomes from these plots are not quite inconsiderable, since they are cultivated more intensively than the farmland that is collectivized. It should be added that in some socialist countries collectivization of agriculture has only been accomplished to a limited extent. Likewise, private income from capital does exist in a modest way in some socialist countries. This of course applies to capital invested in the private farming just referred to. It can be added that in China interest is paid on deposits in the People's Banks.[2]

Hierarchical inequality seems to be rather important in the USSR, but much less in China. In fact, the Cultural Revolution can be seen at least in part as a reaction against an evolution that was feared to be similar to that experienced in the USSR in this respect. China has tried to avoid the establishment of a powerful bureaucracy with relatively high incomes.

More will be said about hierarchical and geographical inequality in Chapter 9. What will happen to geographical inequality is one of the most important questions of the foreseeable future, and especially the inequality between the present LICs and the richer countries.

As regards sectoral inequality, it seems appropriate in the present chapter to have a somewhat closer look at its most important aspect, namely the difference in income levels between agriculture and the rest of the economy. For the world as a whole agriculture is still employing about as many people as all other activities taken together.

By combining the statistics concerning the population engaged in agriculture, with national accounts statistics, it is possible to compare the gross domestic product (GDP per capita in agriculture with that in "nonagriculture." This is done in Table 5.7, where the last column but one indicates the level for GDP per capita in agriculture when the corresponding level for "nonagriculture" is 100. In a similar way the last column shows the level for agriculture in relation to society as a whole, the total economy including agriculture. Of these two indicators, the latter is the one that reflects income distribution in the most general way. If we compare agriculture with society as a whole, the former is poorer in all seven groups, but particularly in Groups 4, 5, and 6. These were also the groups that showed the highest level of the "Gini ratio" in Table 5.5, thus indicating the most unequal income distribution. This special study of agriculture seems to confirm the view expressed earlier in this section, that inequality of income distribution increases in the early stages of a typical development process but decreases in the later stages.

The column "Relative Level I" compares agriculture directly with the nonagricultural sector, assuming we accept a two-sector concept, which is most relevant in countries where most people belong to the agricultural community. This comparison therefore shows to what extent countries are dual societies in the sense described above. If the disparity between the levels of agriculture and "nonagriculture" is very marked, the society in question is close to the pattern shown in Figure 5.2, which is that of a dual society. The table shows that this is true of Group 6 and, if we exclude India and Pakistan, still more of Group 7. It therefore seems to be a general feature of LICs, with the exception of the two big South Asian Countries.

There are in fact more exceptions, as can be seen from Table 5.8, where the countries are arranged according to categories and regions. This table shows that in general Asian countries are much less "dual" in their structure than African countries. Relative Level I is much lower in Africa than in Asia, where in fact its general level is equal to that of most MICs.

The explanation of this important difference can no doubt be found in the historical fact that Asia on the whole has been in the main stream of progress much longer than has the main part of the African continent. Therefore the "modern sector" in Asia is older than that of the typical African state.

TABLE 5.7

Relative Level of GDP in Agriculture, 1970

Group	Number of Countries	Population 1967 (millions)	Agriculture (percent of total) Population	GDP	Relative Level I	II
1	7	297.7	6.5	3.6	53.7	55.4
2	10	225.8	9.8	5.3	51.5	54.1
3	11	443.8	29.3	17.1	49.8	58.4
4	13	155.9	33.9	12.8	28.6	37.7
5	15	208.8	51.2	18.7	21.9	36.5
6	15	291.1	68.6	22.7	13.4	33.0
7	11	725.6	70.4	43.3	32.1	61.5
Total	82	2,348.7	44.4	9.3	12.8	20.9
Group 7: India and Pakistan	9	94.5	84.1	35.4	9.7	40.3

Source: *FAO Production Yearbook 1971* (Rome: Food and Agricultural Organization) and *UN Yearbook of National Accounts Statistics 1971*, Volume III (New York: United Nations).

TABLE 5.8

Relative Level of GDP in Agriculture, by Categories and Regions, 1970

	Number of Countries	Population 1967 (millions)	Agriculture (percent of total) Population	Agriculture (percent of total) GDP	Relative Level I	Relative Level II	Land per Capita of Agricultural Population* (hectares)
HICs	15	518.1	7.9	4.1	49.8	51.9	13.0
North America and Oceania	3	231.3	4.6	3.2	68.6	69.6	42.2
Europe	12	286.8	10.5	5.5	49.6	52.4	2.7
MICs	39	808.5	35.8	16.4	35.2	45.8	2.5
Japan	1	99.9	21.0	7.0	24.7	29.3	0.3
USSR	1	235.5	32.0	22.0	59.9	52.9	43.3
Latin America	17	220.0	40.7	12.8	21.4	31.5	2.0
Other MICs	20	253.1	41.1	16.2	27.7	39.4	2.1
LICs	24	1,008.3	69.9	35.7	23.9	51.1	0.6
Asia	10	883.2	65.8	36.2	26.1	50.8	0.4
Africa	14	125.1	80.2	32.0	11.6	39.9	1.6
Total	78	2,334.9	44.3	9.3	12.9	21.0	1.6

*1 hectare of permanent pasture = ¼ hectare of arable land.

Source: FAO Production Yearbook 1971 (Rome: Food and Agricultural Organization) and UN Yearbook of National Accounts Statistics 1971; Volume III (New York: United Nations).

The Asian modern sector has had time to broaden and spread to some extent, in the form of small-scale industries, even in the rural areas.

Also, Asian agriculture has had time to develop under some influence from abroad, and therefore its economic level is closer to that of the non-agricultural sector than is the case in Africa. In fact, since the general economic level of LICs is the same in the two continents (see Table 4.2), it is remarkable that the level of agriculture in Asia is substantially higher than in Africa in spite of the fact that the farm families in the latter continent have four times as much land per capita as their colleagues in Asia.

As a result of this higher degree of continuity in Asian than in African development, the changes going on today in Asia are on the whole less drastic, and the inequalities of income distribution are less marked. The poverty is just as serious, however, because there is so little land per capita.

Two other features of the picture shown in Table 5.8 should be mentioned. One is that Latin American countries seem to be closer to the pattern of dual societies than most other MICs. In fact, since their colonization by Spain and Portugal many Latin American countries seem to have kept some characteristic features of the feudal societies by which they were conquered. There are still very big agricultural holdings, and to the old upper class of landowners has now been added a class of modern industrialists, to a large extent the result of investments by corporations in the United States. There has been less of the kind of continuous development that creates an indigenous middle class than would have taken place if the descendants of the original power elite had not been able to maintain their position until the present century. There is in this respect some similarity between Latin America and Southern Africa, likewise dominated by the descendants of European emigrants.

The last feature of Table 5.8 to be noted is the marked contrast between North America, Oceania, and the USSR on the one hand and all the other regions on the other, as regards the area per capita of the agricultural population. It is not surprising that the GDP per capita in agriculture is higher in regions with a great deal of land per capita of the agricultural population, than it is in other regions at roughly speaking the same economic level.

The GDP generated in agriculture is of course not identical with the income of the farming population. Part of it goes in various forms to absentee landlords or to moneylenders and banks, especially in the poor countries. On the other hand, many families on the smaller farms in the rich countries get earnings of various kinds from work in the nonagricultural sectors. It would seem likely, therefore, that the difference in real income between agricultural familes in rich and poor countries is even greater than the difference in GDP per capita.

In the sections that follow, various social indicators are considered. Unfortunately, the information available often refers to averages for a whole country, rather than to individual groups within the population. If, say, the average standards of nutrition are different in two countries with the same average income level, one is inclined to draw the conclusion that income distribution must be more unequal in the country with the lower nutritional standard than in the other country. This cannot be proved, but if one studies a number of such social indicators in conjunction with one another the result will yield a relatively coherent picture with important policy implications. Therefore it seems worthwhile to make the effort even at present. The statistical basis is improving, and in some years' time it should be possible to put together a more perfect mosaic than the one presented here.

EMPLOYMENT

The employment problem is another consequence of the process of differentiation. In subsistence agriculture there can be no unemployment; there can be underemployment in the sense that not all of the people are working all of the time, but it is only when differentiation has reached a stage at which some people have to sell their labor on the market that employment versus unemployment becomes an issue.

Nothing will be said in this book about seasonal variations in employment because they have nothing to do with the development process; nor is it the intention here to discuss the effects of booms and depressions on the level of employment. The purpose of this section is rather to discuss briefly the serious unemployment problem in countries that are becoming dual socieities at a certain stage of their development.

This was bound to happen in the present phase of history, in which countries at very different economic levels are increasingly connected because of the instruments of communication and transport that exist today. As discussed in the previous section, in all the poor countries this is leading to the establishment of modern sectors with two characteristics, the first of which is that they are small, and the second that they have much higher income levels than the traditional sectors. They therefore attract much more people from the rural areas than they can employ, resulting in miserable shanty towns, where many of the inhabitants are employed only now and then.

In many LICs there are therefore more really poor people than small farmers and landless laborers. There is also an often rapidly increasing number of unemployed people on the outskirts of the big cities. Because of family solidarity based on old traditions, those who earn an income from work are often supporting those who are without such earnings, and sometimes also their relatives in the villages where they were born. It remains that the special type of unemployment that results from the dual societies of these countries is both a waste of human resources and often a serious problem for a considerable part of the population.

The basic fact about this structural unemployment in dual societies is of course the wide income gap between the modern and traditional sectors, often accompanied by a difference in social status; this tempts too many people to leave the villages in the hope of getting a position within the privileged minority. We can therefore find the explanation of this migration partly in the nature of the two sectors and partly in the illusions of those who move.

The modern sector usually applies techniques that have developed in HICs, where labor is expensive and capital relatively cheap. These techniques often require skills that are rare in the country. Such special technical knowledge may often be required for the more important posts, that they must be filled by people from the home country of the foreign corporation in question. Some of the processes may be performed in a more labor-intensive way than in the home country, but the number of jobs offered in this way will often be rather limited. A further complication is introduced when competition from the modern industry spoils the market for some local crafts, thus destroying more jobs than it creates.

In the traditional sector, and in particular on the small farms, incomes are usually very low. Because of rapid population growth the pressure on the land is increasing in many LICs and also in MICs such as those belonging to Group 7 in Table 4.1. Therefore production will not be reduced much if some people leave for the cities, leaving fewer family members to share the output of the farm. In some LICs much of the field work is done by women. In such countries it is often only men who go to the cities.

Productivity in agriculture and also in rural handicrafts and small-scale industry could be raised by rather simple investment, but it is one of the paradoxes of a dual society that the available capital is channeled chiefly into the modern sector through the banks, which belong to that sector, and of course through direct investment by foreign firms. Even development assistance projects are often in the form of capital intensive undertakings. Meanwhile the small farmers and artisans are forced to seek capital from moneylenders at exorbitant rates of interest.

The people who move to the cities will often have gone to school, whether they have completed primary school education or dropped out after two or three years. Unfortunately this has in most cases not given them the skills that would qualify them for good jobs in the modern sector, since the educational system is often not adapted to the requirements of that sector, nor for that matter to those of the traditional one. This will be a major subject of the section of this chapter on education.

Thus lack of adaptation is at the root of the problem: the modern sector is not adapted to the skills of the majority of the people. Those who leave the village often no longer feel at home in the rural community; when arriving in the cities, however, they find that they are not adapted to the needs of the modern sector either.

It is not surprising that there is such a general disharmony in dual societies, since they represent an encounter between two very different economic and cultural systems. Most people in an LIC are not at all adapted to the institutions established in their country because of its relations with HICs. Only a small minority fulfill that condition; the members of another minority feel bewildered and alienated, not knowing whether they belong to the modern or the traditional community and unable to find appropriate jobs.

Countries that have been in the "main stream of progress" over a longer period usually have a more harmonious social structure. The "modern" sector started long ago and is therefore not so radically different from the other activities of the country, which have had time to develop so that various industries and trades have been able to absorb the manpower released by agriculture.

Something similar should happen eventually in those countries that are dual societies today; but it may take a long time before the structural unemployment begins to go down; and in the meantime it may reach dangerous levels. There is a growing concern about that in many countries, and as a consequence there is an increasing interest in furthering rural development. By this is meant a mixture of policies aimed at keeping people in the rural areas through improvements in agriculture and through the establishment of small-scale industries and such public works as sanitary installations and road construction. There are also efforts to make education more work-oriented and thus more useful for people who are to get their living from work in the rural districts.

It is interesting to note that this is exactly what China has been doing since it became a socialist country. The People's Communes are mixed communities, the occupations in which include agriculture, handicrafts, some industries, education and health service.

There is some similarity between this system and the Kibbutzim in Israel and the Ujama villages in Tanzania. These are all variants of a policy of developing the rural communities, keeping more people there, and offering them employment.

NUTRITION

In this and the following sections in this chapter I shall study some important aspects of the kind of life people in the various parts of the world have been able to lead, earning the incomes I have described in the second section.

The standard of nutrition is no doubt the most fundamental. It is described in Table 5.9 for the usual seven income groups of countries. The picture in this table of the relationship between income level and nutritional standard is very clear. It is particularly marked as regards animal protein, and the spectacular difference between the poorest and the richest group in this field throws some interesting light on the history of mankind during the last 10,000 years.

Some studies seem to indicate that food consumption in various pre-agricultural societies was surprisingly "correct" and well balanced, seen from the point of view of modern medical science. The hunters and food gatherers got a mixed diet composed of things taken from many kinds of plants and animals, big and small, and they must have found out what compositions of such food items were good for them.

When agriculture started, the food supply became more ample and the population began to grow faster, but nutrition also became more one-sided. Grains and other kinds of plant food predominated, at least among the poorer people, and they still do today.

The table clearly indicates, however, that when people can afford a somewhat better standard of living they again decide to have more animal food. In fact, modern nutrition experts have found that in the rich countries we are

TABLE 5.9

Food Consumption per Person per Day, circa 1967

Group	Calories	Animal Protein (grams)	Total Protein (grams)
1	3,170	65.8	95.5
2	3,010	47.4	85.1
3	3,070	35.5	88.1
4	2,740	25.0	76.2
5	2,290	16.8	56.6
6	2,120	10.0	51.3
7	2,020	7.4	53.8
Average	2,400	21.1	65.3

Note: This table covers all of the countries in Table A.1 except Papua and New Guinea.

Source: FAO Production Yearbook 1971 (Rome: Food and Agricultural Organization).

again approaching a pattern of food consumption that in fundamental elements comes close to that of our preagricultural forefathers.

I have mentioned earlier in this book that in a number of respects the seven income groups represent stages in a development process that is actually going on. This is also the case regarding food consumption, as can be seen from Table 5.10.

It is interesting to note that even in the richest group of countries there has been an increase in the consumption of animal protein. Relatively, however, the largest increase in this "wealth indicator" has taken place in the MICs; that is, Groups 3, 4, and 5. That was to be expected, since they have had the most rapid economic growth, but it must of course be confessed that the number of countries covered by Table 5.10 is rather small.

The two countries from Group 7 that are represented in the table are India and Pakistan. In Pakistan there has been a clear improvement in calories and total protein, but the consumption of animal protein was virtually unchanged in 1970 (10 grams, compared with 9.9 grams in 1960). In India the consumption of both calories and protein has gone down, from 6.1 to 5.6 grams as regards animal protein. As mentioned in the second section of this chapter, the explanation no doubt is that income distribution has become more unequal, giving the poorer part of the population a lower standard of living during the decade. The Green Revolution has benefited the larger farmers, but it has no doubt been harmful to the landless laborers, and the rural-urban migration referred to in the previous section has no doubt increased the number of those who live under very poor conditions on the outskirts of the cities, who are unemployed a large part of the time.

Another significant feature of the evolution in India is that the production of pulses has gone down while the area under wheat has increased. This must

TABLE 5.10

Food Consumption per Person per Day, 1960 and 1970

Group	Number of Countries	Population 1967 (millions)	Calories 1960	Calories 1970	Animal Protein (grams) 1960	Animal Protein (grams) 1970	Total Protein (grams) 1960	Total Protein (grams) 1970
1	7	280.1	3,120	3,260	62.2	67.8	93.2	97.7
2	8	204.3	3,000	3,020	45.3	49.8	83.5	86.3
3	3	113.0	2,420	2,540	24.9	31.6	73.1	77.6
4	3	42.8	2,740	2,740	24.7	35.6	76.1	82.1
5	1	13.1	1,870	2,620	15.3	20.9	58.5	68.2
6	2	46.4	2,040	2,050	15.2	17.1	47.5	50.7
7	2	631.1	2,040	2,020	6.8	6.4	50.3	49.0
Total	26	1,330.8	2,470	2,510	26.9	29.6	67.2	68.7

Source: FAO Production Yearbook 1971 (Rome: Food and Agricultural Organization).

also be considered a consequence of the Green Revolution, which made it profitable to extend the cultivation of high-yielding Mexican wheat.

It can be added that the very low consumption of animal protein is a general feature of Asia, more than Africa. (See Table 5.11.) It is particularly the low level for India and Indonesia that has brought the overall figure for Asia down. For India this has also to do with the Hindu practice of not killing cows and therefore not eating beef. However, in China the consumption of animal protein per person per day was also substantially lower than in Africa, namely 7.9 grams.

Those countries where part of the population still lives in nomadic communities have contributed particularly to the relatively high figure for Africa. Thus, the consumption of animal protein per person per day was 18.7 grams in Sudan and 22.2 in Somalia. There is more land per capita in Africa than in Asia, and therefore there is a possibility of having more livestock..

In Latin American countries the figures for animal protein are slightly higher than those for other MICs, while the opposite is true for calories and for total protein. The reason for that is no doubt to be found in the high level of meat consumption in those South American countries where beef cattle are raised on a large scale. Thus the daily consumption of animal protein was 59.8 grams in Argentina and 71.8 grams in Uruguay, but for the rest of Latin America the standard was much lower.

The standard of food consumption was considerably higher in the USSR than in Japan, although GNP per capita was slightly lower. The reason is probably that Japan is an Asian country and is therefore still influenced by old Asian eating habits, while the USSR is closer to European traditions. It must be added, though, that consumption of animal food has been growing fast in

TABLE 5.11

Food Consumption, per Person per Day, by Categories and Regions, circa 1967

	Calories	Animal Protein (grams)	Total Protein (grams)
HICs	3,110	58.0	90.8
North America and Oceania	3,200	68.0	95.6
Europe	3,030	50.2	87.2
MICs	2,710	27.5	77.0
Japan	2,450	28.3	74.7
USSR	3,180	35.8	92.2
Latin America	2,520	24.5	65.2
Other MICs	2,610	23.4	75.7
LICs	2,040	7.9	51.3
Asia	2,010	7.6	52.2
Africa	2,230	9.9	45.7
Total	2,390	21.1	64.5

Source: FAO Production Yearbook 1971 (Rome: Food and Agricultural Organization).

Japan. The figure for animal protein was 22.8 in 1960, but 29.7 in 1970. The same phenomenon can be noted in other MICs with rapid economic growth; in Spain the corresponding increase was from 24 to 36.9, and in Libya from 9.3 to 17.8.

There are four conclusions one can draw from this study of food consumption:

1. With rising income levels the consumption of animal food increases rapidly, especially at medium income levels.

2. As in other fields, the really important gap is between MICs and LICs, and the gap is widening.

3. The nutritional standard is particularly low in Asia, which is densely populated.

4. If income distribution becomes more unequal, as it often seems to do in the earlier stages of development, nutrition may become poorer even if there is some increase in the average level of GNP per capita.

If to this we add the well-known fact that there is widespread malnutrition in many poor countries, it becomes obvious that the problem of nutrition will be one of great concern in the foreseeable future.

HOUSING

Information about the housing situation of the world's population is very incomplete, and it is not possible to undertake a real statistical analysis as in the case of food consumption. One of the reasons, of course, is that the quality of a house cannot be measured. Though calories and quantities of protein are only imperfect indicators of the quantity and quality of food, they do nevertheless permit, between countries, comparisons that show a considerable degree of regularity and therefore are of some interest. There is nothing by which standards of housing can be compared in a similar way.

Another important fact about housing is that in many of the poorer countries a large part of the rural population, as well as people in the urban slums, build their own houses. There is therefore no price mechanism by which the value of houses in various countries or regions can be compared. This is not to say that quantitative information is nonexistent. A good general description of the situation and of recent development is given in the 1970 *Report on the World Social Situation* of the United Nations.[3] The following considerations are to a large extent built on information contained in this report.

It contains an estimate[4] according to which there was a housing deficit in Latin America of 20 million units and in Asia (apart from China and a few other countries) of 147 million units in 1960. Such estimates are of course always open to doubt. Of a more general nature is the statement contained in the Introduction that

> while the housing situation in more developed regions has generally improved or maintained approximate stability, it has elsewhere declined sharply from he already inadequate levels prevailing in earlier years and, in the wake of rapid population growth, has led to a vast expansion of squatter settlements and urban and rural slums.[5]

This statement is interesting because it focuses attention on exactly those parts of the population that are the victims of rising inequality of income distribution, namely, the unemployed in the slums around the cities and the poorer part of the farming population.

The report contains a few quantitative estimates about the annual number of dwellings built per thousand inhabitants.[6] It is said that in most developing countries this is less than two, compared with the following figures for some richer countries and regions:

	Number of Dwellings per Thousand Residents
United States	8.0
Western Europe	7.0
Eastern Europe	5.7
USSR	9.4
Japan	11.9

Although it is not clear to what extent self-built houses are included in the figure for developing countries, it seems clear that the gap is widening. It must be remembered that population growth is much faster in the poorer countries than in the richer ones.

To this can be added some figures about the estimated population in so-called "uncontrolled settlements," in percent of the city population in some important cities:

	Percent of Population in "Uncontrolled Settlements"
Dakar, Dar-es-Salaam, Lusaka	30
Calcutta, Karachi, Manila	35
Colombo	44
Recife, Mexico City	46-50
Ankara, Izmir	60

About Asia it is stated[7] that the only countries in which low income housing conditions improved during the 1960s are Japan, Hong Kong, and Singapore. It is also indicated that house construction includes "disproportionately high investment in quality private housing for the rich." The general picture concerning urban housing is described as one of rapid decline.

Another section of the report deals with water supply in rural areas. Here it is said, "In developing countries it has been calculated that the proportion of rural dwellers served with safe water is in the neighbourhood of 10 percent."[8]

In fairness it must be added that there is an increasing awareness of the serious housing situation in a number of the poorer countries. Programs of low-cost housing that utilize materials from the natural resources of the countries in question are being devised. So far, however, progress has been slow.

In spite of its uncertainty the general picture that emerges from the information available seems to be rather clear. It points to a dangerously bad and often deteriorating situation regarding housing for the same groups of people we have found in bad situations in other respects. They are the people with the lowest incomes in the LICs and the lower brackets of the MICs. If they are farmers they have too little land; if not, they are often unemployed, and their nutrition as well as their habitation is poor.

ENERGY CONSUMPTION

The consumption of energy is linked partly to the production process in agriculture, industry, and transports, and partly to the creation of such comforts as heating, air conditioning, and lighting. Other things being equal, therefore, energy consumption will be at a higher level in cold climates than in the tropics, but on the whole it is a fairly good indicator of the economic level of a country, as can be seen from Table 5.12.

TABLE 5.12

Energy Consumption, 1961 and 1970
(coal equivalent)

	Total Consumption		Annual Growth 1961-70 (percent)	Annual Growth of GNP 1960-70 (percent)	Consumption 1970 (kilograms)	
Group	(millions of tons) 1961	1970			Per Capita	Per Dollar of GNP
1	1,807.4	2,859.6	5.2	4.6	9,063	2.14
2	780.3	1,140.0	4.3	4.3	4,686	1.99
3	955.1	1,729.6	6.7	7.8	3,777	2.25
4	152.5	272.0	6.6	6.7	1,572	2.06
5	87.3	186.2	8.8	5.7	569	1.54
6	47.9	95.4	8.0	5.2	235	1.45
7	347.6	529.3	4.8	3.9	305	2.48
Total	4,178.1	6,812.1	5.6	5.3	1,861	2.12

Note: This table covers all of the countries in Table A.1 except Taiwan and Yemen.

Source: United Nations, *World Energy Supplies 1961-1970* (New York: the UN, 1972).

As a general rule energy consumption increased at the same speed as GNP during the 1960s. Its growth was, however, substantially faster than GNP growth in the three poorest income groups, and this is not surprising. When a society begins to develop "modern" activities and ways of life, consumption of energy is bound to increase.

If we look at the three main categories of countries as shown in Table 5.13, we therefore find that the really important gap is the one between MICs and LICs. Since energy is likely to become much more expensive than in the 1960s it is a serious question to what extent this will hamper a further development of the poorest countries. I will come back to this important problem in Chapter 9, but there are a couple of special features of the picture shown in Table 5.13 that should be commented on now.

As could be expected, the level of energy consumption was much lower in Africa than in Asia, where the modern sector has a broader base because it has developed over a longer period. The relatively low level of energy consumption in Latin America may well have to do with the fact already mentioned, that the industrial base in this region is relatively narrow. Once more, therefore, we see an indication of similarity between Africa and Latin America. Both seem to be dual societies to a greater extent than other regions at the same economic level.

In considering Tables 5.12 and 5.13, one should take into account that until the early 1970s the prices of energy, and of oil in particular, had been falling in relation to prices in general. As they rise in comparison with other prices, it can be expected that energy consumption will begin to grow more

TABLE 5.13

Energy Consumption, by Categories and Regions, 1961 and 1970
(coal equivalent)

	Total Consumption		Annual Growth	Annual Growth of GNP	Consumption 1970 (kilograms)	
	(millions of tons)		1961-70	1960-70	Per	Per Dollar
	1961	1970	(percent)	(percent)	Capita	of GNP
HICs	2,581.2	3,984.2	4.9	4.5	7,203	2.10
North America and Oceania	1,630.4	2,547.1	5.1	4.5	10,543	2.32
Europe	950.8	1,437.1	4.7	4.5	4,613	1.80
MICs	1,194.9	2,187.8	7.0	7.4	2,284	2.14
Japan	123.4	332.4	11.6	10.7	3,215	1.67
USSR	630.8	1,076.9	7.3	7.1	4,435	2.48
Latin America	140.2	231.5	5.7	5.3	873	1.55
Other MICs	300.5	547.0	6.9	7.1	1,579	2.28
LICs	394.8	623.5	5.2	4.3	292	2.24
Asia	375.8	593.6	5.2	4.3	321	2.49
Africa	19.0	29.9	5.2	4.4	107	0.76
Total	4,170.9	6,812.1	5.6	5.3	1,869	2.13

Source: United Nations, *World Energy Supplies 1961-1970* (New York: the UN, 1972).

slowly. The question is, of course, whether this new development will influence the comfort of people in the rich countries more than the essential activities in the poor countries, or vice versa. This difficult problem will be considered in Chapter 9.

HEALTH

The health situation of a population depends mainly on two factors. In a general way it depends on the living conditions, especially the standards of nutrition and housing. And then of course it depends in a more specific way on the health services directly available. The health standard of a country is therefore to a large extent the result of its development in the fields discussed in the previous sections, such as income level and distribution, nutrition, housing, and to some extent energy consumption.

There is in this respect, as in so many others, a significant difference between countries that have been in the "main stream of progress" for a long time and those that have been drawn into it more recently and more abruptly, by the transfer of modern technology.

In the former the general health situation has improved slowly for centuries, and in the earlier phases of this development it was due to improved nutrition and other living conditions more than to direct health service. Thus, in the first part of the 19th century the health situation in at least some of the bigger European cities was substantially worse than in the countryside because the crowded urban population was more exposed to infectious disease. The spectacular progress in medical science has had its major effects on health only in a rather recent phase of the development of HICs.

At the other extreme, most LICs have only experienced a marked progress during the last generation or so, and this was due to the introduction of modern health services more than to an improvement in nutrition or housing. Thus, in these countries the fight against epidemics has preceded a significant improvement of living conditions, while it was the other way around in countries that benefited from a longer and more continuous process of social change.

It is a fairly hopeless task to measure the health standard of a country. Statistics about many kinds of illness do exist, but there is no objective way to weigh one against another. What one can do is measure the efforts in terms of health service and then a couple of indicators of life and death. If the average lifetime becomes longer, and if the infant mortality rates go down, it is fair to conclude that the general health standard has improved. Table 5.14 described some major elements of the health service of countries in the seven income groups during the 1960s.

As could be expected, the relative numbers of health service personnel increase when we move upwards through the income scale. The high level for Group 3 is mainly because of the large number of physicians and nurses in the USSR, which had more physicians per 10,000 inhabitants than any other country except Israel.

As a result of the various factors mentioned, the expectation of life increases in a rather regular way from the lowest to the highest of the seven income groups of countries in Table 5.15, except that there is virtually no progress from Group 3 onwards; this has to do with a phenomenon that appears even more clearly in Table 5.16, describing the various regions. Although the first region, North America and Oceania, has a substantially higher income level than Europe, its life extectancy is slightly lower. In fact, life expectancy for men has gone down in some rich countries. Automobile accidents and the stress created by some kinds of life in a modern society are probably the main causes. This is one of the disquieting aspects of recent developments in HICs; others will be mentioned in later parts of this book. Taken together they demonstrate that the income level is by no means a sure measure of the standard of living. They also have some implications for the considerations about the future contained in Chapter 9.

Apart from this particular phenomenon there is nothing surprising in Table 5.16. It is worth noting that expectation of life is somewhat higher in Asia than in Africa.

TABLE 5.14

**Health Service Personnel
per 10,000 Population**

Group	Physicians			Nurses			Paramedical Personnel		
	Number of Countries	Population 1967 (millions)	Personnel	Number of Countries	Population 1967 (millions)	Personnel	Number of Countries	Population 1967 (millions)	Personnel
1	9	306.6	14.5	5	265.5	45.3	7	295.7	5.2
2	11	238.4	15.3	9	168.9	34.1	8	166.1	4.1
3	11	443.8	18.0	10	424.5	40.2	8	176.3	4.0
4	15	160.9	8.5	11	111.1	15.9	14	159.3	1.4
5	25	286.6	3.5	16	223.3	5.9	18	236.0	0.5
6	22	341.5	2.2	21	340.4	4.6	17	330.1	1.0
7	23	860.4	1.6	22	855.1	2.7	7	622.7	0.7
Average	116	2,638.2	7.8	94	2,388.8	17.5	79	1,986.2	2.0

Source: World Health Organization, *World Health Statistics Annual*, Vol. III, 1968.

TABLE 5.15

Expectation of Life at Birth*

Group	Number of Countries	Population 1967 (millions)	Average Expectancy
1	9	306.6	70.9
2	11	238.4	70.8
3	11	443.8	69.9
4	14	158.4	63.6
5	24	286.9	55.6
6	25	369.2	49.7
7	22	1,564.9	45.9
Total	116	3,368.2	55.2

*Figures refer to various years in the decade 1960-70.

Source: UN Demographic Yearbook 1970 (New York: United Nations).

TABLE 5.16

Expectation of Life at Birth, by Categories and Regions

	Number of Countries	Population 1967 (millions)	Average Expectancy
HICs	18	539.6	70.8
North America and Oceania	4	234.1	70.5
Europe	14	305.5	71.1
MICs	49	889.1	64.2
Japan	1	99.9	71.7
USSR	1	235.5	70.0
Latin America	20	245.1	60.1
Other MICs	27	308.6	60.5
LICs	45	1,925.7	46.6
Asia	18	1,680.6	47.3
Africa	27	245.1	41.5
Total	112	3,354.4	55.2

Source: UN Demographic Yearbook 1970 (New York: United Nations).

The situation is different, however, concerning infant mortality, another important health indicator. The infant mortality rates given in Table 5.17 show how many out of every 1,000 children born, die before reaching the age of one year. The table shows the same two general features that we have found for most of the other social indicators. There was progress during the decade for all seven income groups of countries, and there is improvement when we move upwards from the lowest to the highest group. There is, however, some inequality concerning the lower income groups, but it should be remembered that it has been possible to cover only a few of the countries in these groups.

If we look at the various geographical regions, some interesting additional information is obtained, as shown in Table 5.18.

The remarkably low figure for Japan in 1970 may have something to do with the fact that induced abortion is used to a rather considerable extent in that country, and quite a number of births may have been prevented that would have taken place under circumstances that were socially unfavorable. It would be worthwhile to have the Japanese development in this field studied by experts, since abortion by intervention is now becoming more common in other countries as well.

One spectacular feature of the table is the high level of infant mortality in Latin America compared with other MICs; since most Latin American countries are covered by the table, this can be no statistically misleading presentation. The explanation may at least partly be found in the fact mentioned earlier that in general Latin American countries are dual societies to a higher degree than other countries at the same economic level; this means that a large part of the population lives under socially unfavorable circumstances. It is in conformity with the fact mentioned earlier that, apart from a couple of beef-producing

TABLE 5.17

Infant Mortality

Group	Number of Countries	Population 1967 (millions)	Infant Mortality per 1,000 1960	Infant Mortality per 1,000 1970
1	9	306.6	25.3	18.5
2	11	238.4	32.0	22.6
3	10	442.1	39.2	26.2
4	13	140.4	67.9	51.4
5	13	78.2	91.5	75.2
6	8	138.8	77.8	62.6
7	2	515.8	146.8	138.8
Total	66	1,860.3	73.1	62.4

Source: UN Demographic Yearbook 1961 and 1970 (New York: United Nations).

TABLE 5.18

Infant Mortality, by Categories and Regions

	Number of Countries	Population 1967 (millions)	Infant Mortality per 1,000 1960	1970
HICs	18	539.6	28.2	20.8
North America and Oceania	4	234.1	25.4	20.9
Europe	14	305.5	30.2	20.7
MICs	36	660.7	51.5	37.4
Japan	1	99.9	30.7	13.1
USSR	1	235.5	35.0	24.4
Latin America	17	149.2	80.6	65.6
Other MICs	17	176.1	60.7	44.6
LICs	10	654.6	131.8	123.1
Asia	6	613.6	131.6	124.4
Africa	4	41.0	135.2	104.0
Total	64	1,854.9	73.1	62.8

Source: UN Demographic Yearbook 1961 and *1970* (New York: United Nations).

countries, the nutritional standard of Latin American countries is lower than that of other MICs.

According to Table 5.18 there has been more progress in Africa than in Asia, which shows the highest infant mortality rate for 1970. Only ten LICs are represented in this table, but it is possible to get much more information for the year 1970 only. For that year statistics exist for nine Asian countries, with a total population in 1967 of 849.3 million, and for twenty-three African countries with a population of 173.0 million. The infant mortality rates were 124.8 and 110.6, respectively. The rates were particularly high for the big countries; Indonesia had a rate of 125, India had 139, and Pakistan had 142.

How are these figures compatible with the figures in Table 5.16, which show life expectancy to be higher in Asia than in Africa? In that table China was included, and with a life expectancy of 50 years it of course raises the average. Even apart from China the average lifetime was higher in Asia than in Africa, however.

It is important to carry this analysis of infant mortality as far as possible because, as I shall argue in Chapter 6, a considerable reduction of infant mortality is probably the only factor that can bring birth rates down in an important way. When people become convinced that children are now surviving much more often than before, they will gradually reduce their procreation whether they have heard about family planning or not.

I think the apparent contradiction between the two series of vital statistics considered above can be explained in the following way. Life expectancy depends on many aspects of living conditions and also to a large extent on the quality of the available health services. Therefore it has reached a higher level in Asia than in Africa because Asia has had a longer, broader and more continuous participation in the main stream of progress than has Africa. Infant mortality, on the other hand, depends more on the standard of nutrition, particularly for pregnant women and nursing mothers. Therefore its levels are higher in Asia than in Africa because nutritional standards are lower, as shown in the fourth section of this chapter.

This has serious implications for future development. As already mentioned, the low standard of nutrition in Asia has to do with the scarcity of land. This scarcity will be increasing in the decades to come, and it is therefore to be feared that infant mortality rates will remain high for a rather long period. As a consequence the birth rates may also remain rather high, so that population growth rates will go down only slowly. There is here a kind of vicious circle, which may well represent one of the major development problems of the foreseeable future. More will therefore be said about it in Chapter 6 and 9.

EDUCATION

In view of what has been said in Chapters 2 and 3 about the importance of knowledge as a factor of development, it is of particular interest to study how knowledge spreads through the process of education.

This process requires an effort on the part of pupils as well as teachers, and it takes a number of years for children and adults to acquire and digest a reasonable part of the enormous stock of knowledge existing today. Only if relevant knowledge is digested through a long process of learning and reflection does it become an integral part of one's personality. On the other hand, few things are changing men and women more than this longish process, by which they are gradually becoming partners in that great fund of knowledge that is the common property of mankind.

It follows that statistics can give only an imperfect picture of the social change generated by the system of education. Figures can describe the teaching offered but not really the kind of learning resulting from it. Statistics are, of course, essential for an evaluation of the development going on, provided we are aware of the necessity for supplementary considerations that cannot always be quantified.

Table 5.19 describes the development in the 1960s in enrollment ratios for primary, secondary, and higher education in the seven income groups of countries. Roughly speaking this table confirms the impression one gets from

TABLE 5.19

School Enrollment Ratios*

Group	First Level 1960	First Level 1969	Second Level 1960	Second Level 1969	Third Level 1960	Third Level 1969
1	110	111	74	90	24.1	37.5
2	116	117	54	69	7.7	13.5
3	103	103	59	67	9.4	20.3
4	84	96	23	37	4.5	6.3
5	77	100	11	23	1.7	4.2
6	68	80	11	20	2.7	5.8
7	38	50	8	13	1.4	2.3
Average	74	84	30	39	6.5	11.6

*Number of students enrolled in comparison to size of age group.

Note: The number of countries covered varies to some extent between the columns of the table. China is not included, but apart from that, the countries of Table A.1 are covered with few exceptions.

Source: UNESCO Statistical Yearbook 1971 (Paris: UNESCO).

considering other social indicators. The evolution in time for all groups corresponds to a movement upwards through the income scale.

A picture with some significant variations is obtained when one studies the main regions of the world as shown in Table 5.20. The enrollment rate for higher education is particularly high in the United States, with 48.1 in 1970. Second in this respect is the USSR, closely followed by Canada and New Zealand. It seems reasonable to conclude that this has had something to do with the competition between the United States and the USSR in military technology and in space research. The increase in the USSR during the 1960s is spectacular.

It is worth noting that the level for secondary education is lower in Latin American than in other MICs, although the level for primary education is higher. This is probably an indicator of the dual-society nature of Latin American communities in addition to those already mentioned. Secondary education can to some extent be considered a typical middle class phenomenon, and it is characteristic of dual societies that there is only a small middle class.

The most important lesson to be drawn from Table 5.20 is, however, that in this as in so many other fields the decisive gap is the one existing between MICs and LICs. The MICs are coming rather close to the level of HICs as regards primary education, but the LICs are still far behind. This is particularly

TABLE 5.20

School Enrollment Ratios, by Categories and Regions

	First Level		Second Level		Third Level	
	1960	1969	1960	1969	1960	1969
HICs	113	114	66	81	17.0	27.0
North America and Oceania	104	111	81	95	29.4	44.3
Europe	121	116	53	69	7.6	13.8
MICs	92	101	38	48	6.2	12.4
Japan	102	99	79	88	8.6	15.8
USSR	104	105	60	67	11.0	26.5
Latin America	92	111	15	27	3.1	6.0
Other MICs	78	91	24	37	3.8	6.4
LICs	46	59	9	15	1.8	2.8
Asia	48	62	11	17	1.9	3.6
Africa	38	46	4	9	1.0	1.2
Average	74	84	30	39	6.6	11.6

Source: UNESCO Statistical Yearbook 1971 (Paris: UNESCO).

true in Africa, where the development process is less advanced than in Asia as regards education, as it is in a number of other fields.

There is one important question about development to which the two tables do not give an answer. To what extent is the educational system adapted to the needs and situations of the countries in question? There are few fields, if any, in which the general problem of adaptation is so closely related to the very nature of human life, as it is in the realm of teaching and learning.

Education is more than a transmission of knowledge; it is also a preparation for life. In this sense education existed long before the act of writing was invented. Parents have always taught their children how to work in the fields and in the house; they have told them about their experiences in life in the village; and they have given them a part in the traditions of the family and the tribe, as well as importing their ideas about religion and about human relations.

This is an informal type of education, closely related to the nature of the society in question. In modern societies it has been supplemented by more and more sophisticated formal education, which has increasingly replaced the old parent-child transmission of experience.

When such a formal system of education, grown out of the needs of highly industrialized HICs, is transferred to poor countries that are largely dominated by subsistence agriculture, we obviously get discontinuity and disharmony. Such a transfer from European countries started in the colonial period, and it has continued in many LICs since independence. At the beginning it was confined to a small minority, but for obvious reasons the governments of the newly independent countries wanted to spread the benefits of education to the whole population as soon as possible. Since nothing else was available they were forced to spread elements of an educational system designed for societies very different from their own.

This is one of the most important aspects of the dual nature of these societies today. It has contributed to the lack of harmony that is characteristic of some of them. Often education has spread faster than available resources indicate; primary education, therefore, is often poor, and many pupils drop out after two or three years, wasting much of the effort. Also, those who have completed school often find it difficult to utilize the knowledge acquired because it is not adapted to the needs of the labor market, as described in the section about employment.

These facts are well known. I think, however, that far too little attention has been paid to another aspect of the situation, which is that while much effort is made to develop formal education for the next generation, very little is done in many countries to help the great majority of adults who have never gone to school. The adults of today, including the youth, will have to do the main part of the work during the next two or three decades; it is therefore essential that they get at least some knowledge about the changing pattern of activities that will characterize their countries during that period.

The dimensions of this problem will become clear through a look at the statistics on illiteracy that are presented in Table 5.21. This table shows the close relationship between literacy and income level that one would expect.

Table 5.22, describing the regional differences, is in conformity with the picture of school enrollment given in Table 5.20. The high level of illiteracy for Africa, of course, reflects the disturbing situation of dual societies.

Table 5.23, in which the various parts of the world are grouped in a slightly different way, illustrates the development in this important field during the decade from 1960 to 1970.

It will be seen that the total number of illiterate adults has increased somewhat during the decade. It is also worth noting that though the percentage is highest for Africa, the number of illiterates in Asia is very large, and progress has been slow in both continents.

Adult illiteracy remains a very serious problem, the worse because it represents a generation gap between children who have gone to school and parents who have not. This is an important aspect of the disharmonious cultural situation in many countries.

In fairness it must be added that there is an increasing awareness in a number of LICs of the lack of adaptation of education to the situation of the societies concerned. Experiments are being made in various countries, supported by international organizations. Since this question of educational

TABLE 5.21

Illiteracy, circa 1960

Group	Number of Countries	Population 1967 (millions)	Percent 15 Years and Older Illiterate
1	1	199.1	2.2
2	3	57.8	10.1
3	7	104.5	12.0
4	14	158.4	28.4
5	20	255.1	48.1
6	15	311.2	51.7
7	12	779.0	75.3
Total	72	1,865.1	50.3

Note: Not included are most HICs, Japan, USSR, and China.
Source: UN Demographic Yearbook 1970 (New York: United Nations).

TABLE 5.22

Illiteracy, by Categories and Regions, circa 1960

	Number of Countries	Population 1967 (millions)	Percent 15 Years and over Illiterate
HICs	2	251.5	3.7
North America and Oceania	1	199.1	2.2
Europe	1	52.4	9.1
MICs	41	518.0	34.8
Japan	—	—	—
USSR	—	—	—
Latin America	19	244.1	32.2
Other MICs	22	273.9	37.2
LICs	25	1,081.8	68.5
Asia	12	915.4	65.5
Africa	13	166.4	84.8
Total	68	1,851.3	50.3

Source: UN Demographic Yearbook 1970 (Paris: UNESCO).

TABLE 5.23

Illiteracy, 1960 and 1970

	Illiterate Adults (millions)		Illiteracy (percent)	
	1960	1970	1960	1970
North America	3.3	2.5	2.4	1.5
Oceania	1.2	1.4	11.5	10.3
Europe and USSR	24.5	18.7	5.3	3.6
Latin America	40.0	38.6	32.5	23.6
Asia*	542.0	579.0	55.2	46.8
Africa	124.0	143.0	81.0	73.7
World	735.0	783.2	39.3	34.2

*Excluding China, North Korea, and North Vietnam.
Source: UNESCO Statistical Yearbook 1971.

adaptation is one of the most crucial problems of the future, it will be discussed further in Chapter 9.

CULTURAL DEVELOPMENT

In a more complete general theory of development there would no doubt be a chapter on the role of culture in the development process. In the present essay, which is only meant as an approach to such a theory, something more modest is appropriate. On the other hand it is essential that the cultural aspect of development be taken into account, since there is such a lively and complicated interaction between cultural and other factors in the process of social change.

What should we understand by the word culture? It is used by different authors with different meanings, but I think it is possible to distinguish between two general types of definition; the word culture can be used in a wider and a narrower sense.

The word culture used in the wider sense is usually understood to refer to the way people are living. This includes their activities in work and leisure, their habits and ideas, their use of tools and houses, and so on. In this sense a description of a certain culture becomes a description of the whole life of the society concerned; this is how social anthropologists write about preagricultural communities.

In this book it is more useful to think of culture in the narrower sense of the ideas, values, rules, and norms that people take over from earlier generations and try to convey to the next generation, with or without modifications. It therefore includes the ideas they have about right or wrong and about religion and the meaning of life. It finds its expressions in arts and literature and also in the habits of the ordinary people, including their attitudes toward foreigners and their behavior.

Man's culture in this narrower sense is of course strongly influenced by the material conditions under which he is living. When these conditions change, ideas and attitudes will also change, but slowly and sometimes after a painful period of conflict between the defenders of tradition and those of new ways of thinking.

In order to understand the cultural situation of the world today, one must remember that until a century or two ago most societies were predominantly agricultural. The vast majority of people were leading a life in close contact with their domestic animals. They were strongly dependent on the changing weather conditions, on which they had no influence. Religions and philosophies in agrarian societies have been marked by strong feelings about what was proper or improper under such circumstances. About the Indians of Latin America it has been said that they had a feeling of inexorable fate, accompanied by humility and melancholy and also by a stoic acceptance of suffering.[9] Similarly, it has been said about the Africans that "the ideal for them . . . has been conformity to the life of one's fellows, seeking little or no wealth and position."[10]

Both in Africa and in Asia the religious status of the cow has been an essential feature of traditional culture. In Asia this applies not only to India, where the cow has been considered a sacred animal but also to China. In Chinese villages cattle "have been classified as members of the household and have a day set aside for the celebration of their birthdays."[11] The members of African pastoral tribes "name themselves after their cattle, compose songs for them, spend their leisure contemplating them, form personal attachments to them."[12]

How different from these traditional cultures is that of the modern business executive, technician, or scientist from Europe or North America who enters into contact with people in Africa, Asia, or Latin America, whether to do business or to give advice. A wide cultural gap often so isolates the Westerner that an intermediary is necessary to interpret his or her knowledge so that it can be received by the nationals of the country, and also to explain their ways of thinking and feeling in return.

One of the great problems of our time is that this encounter of very different cultures is unavoidable. Much harm can be done if those responsible for it do not show sufficient understanding. The main responsibility is that of the representative of an HIC, who has had access to the whole stock of modern knowledge. This includes knowledge about the cultural background of those who are opposite in a negotiation and of the traditional village-dwellers behind them. All too often the HIC representative has not had time—or taken the time needed —to become reasonably well acquainted with this cultural background.

Here there is a serious question to which there is no easy answer. We should meet the ancient cultures with respect and understanding, even with humility; but it would be irresponsible to dissimulate the fact that they are bound to change in the process of further development. The increasing population pressure in many LICs leaves no escape from a progressive transformation of their societies, technically, economically, and socially. When people in these countries have to live under such changing circumstances, their ideas about life and about the world will change. This will be a painful process in many cases, but there is no way back and no possibility for a standstill.

This encounter between two cultures may be facilitated if it takes place through two intermediaries, one from either side, who know something about one another's background and difficulties. Many people from Asia, Africa, and Latin America have had a Western type of education, and not a small number of them are living in Western countries. This intercourse could become the mission of some of these persons, who may see this dilemma upon going home and take up the task of cultural interpreters, in collaboration with opposite numbers from HICs who have sufficient humility to understand that they are coming to MICs or LICs not only to teach, but also to learn, and in particular to learn how to teach without doing harm.

One thing might enhance this understanding, and that is a recognition of the fact that no LIC of today should try to adopt the present culture of any HIC. Indeed, a cultural upheaval is going on in Western countries, and it is very unclear what the outcome will be. The values of yesterday are being questioned, and there is a search for new ideas—or for old ones that might serve under new circumstances. There is a new interest in Western countries in Buddhism, Hinduism, Islam, and other religions of a non-Western origin. If the present encounter of cultures will lead to a new serenity at a later stage, it will certainly not be through the domination of one culture over the others. Cultural development is a voyage under sealed orders.

POLITICAL DEVELOPMENT

The development of political institutions would deserve a full chapter of its own in any really general theory of development, in the same way as the evolution of cultural patterns. Such a chapter would make the study of political structures an integral part of the analysis of social structures and of social change. As an approach to such a study I shall make some comments on the interaction between political systems and ideologies on the one hand, and economic and social change on the other.

Early agrarian societies did not need much political organization. More or less elaborate systems of cooperation were organized in village communities, however, especially where there was a kind of communal ownership of land. This went particularly far when irrigation systems were set up, as in the big river valleys, where the first urban civilizations were later established as well. These were the real birthplace of political organization. The concentration of a fairly large population in crowded cities in fact required such organization, which in turn concentrated powers and wealth in a political system, headed by a monarch. These systems, more than the tribal organizations in various rural areas, are the forerunners of the modern national state. They also started imperialism, extending their influence over new cities and over the surrounding rural areas.[13]

This political system of the Urban Revolution continued in the city-states of ancient Greece, which were also marked by imperialistic features, and it reached a remarkable level of strength in the Roman Empire.

During the centuries after the fall of Rome, the modern national state developed slowly in Western Europe. There is no need to follow its history here, but there are good reasons for examining the relationship between the major phases of this political evolution and the economic and social development that took place at the same time.

In the last section of Chapter 2 it was stressed that during the long period when agriculture was the dominating economic activity, land was the dominant factor of production, and the land-owning aristocracy was a powerful ruling class. Often the kings were strongly dependent on this aristocracy and on the leading persons of the Catholic Church, also a big landowner.

With the growing importance of commerce, shipping, and industry, capital gradually became a source of income and power, later to replace land as the dominant factor. It is of course no accident that the capital-owning bourgeoisie then gradually became a strong political factor, such as they were in Europe in the 19th century. The bourgeoisie also included an important element of the new and growing class of nonclerical intellectuals.

This rise of the bourgeoisie was part of the impact on the political system of the Scientific, Maritime, and Industrial Revolutions that were discussed in Chapter 3.

In the meantime the Egalitarian Revolution was beginning to evolve; its first political result was the creation of the United States of America. This was no revolt against the European domination of people of other races; that came in a later stage in the process: what happened was that a new society of European emigrants broke away from the old European kingdom and formed its own republic.

In the social field the Egalitarian Revolution found a truly revolutionary expression in the socialist theories. It is understandable that they arose exactly at that point in the evolutionary process at which the landowning aristocracy was still in a strong position in many countries and at which the new capital-owning bourgeoisie was gaining strength. The peasant and the emerging class of industrial workers were living in the shadow of these two upper classes. This is probably the period in the history of Western Europe when inequality was the greatest.

Since then the investment of more and more capital for the application of more and more knowledge has increased the productivity of labor. At the same time, land reform and the development of the corporation and the banking system have reduced the power of the big landowners and capitalists. Peasants and workers are therefore in a much stronger position today.

This economic and social development has had its political corollary in a number of important changes in the system, and these changes again have facilitated economic and social reform. Political democracy, universal suffrage, the progressive income tax, and comprehensive social security measures are the main results of this evolution, which has further enhanced the movement towards greater equality.

No doubt these are the reasons why no Western European country has introduced the socialist system. On the other hand, the Western systems are not truly capitalist either; through taxation, monopoly control, and large public investments, the ownership of capital has to some extent been transferred to society as such, and the strict concept of private ownership has been attenuated.

On the other continents, those countries that are former European colonies have to a large extent adopted the political systems that came out of this development in Western Europe. In some of these countries the system is called socialist, but this is often more of a declaration of intent than a description of the real situation existing in the society concerned.

Where the socialist revolution has been carried through in accordance with Marxist philosophy is in Russia and China. It is interesting to note that this happened at points of time at which these two countries were at about the same stage of their economic and social developments as Western Europe was when the socialist theories first appeared. In both countries there was still an old class of big landlords, as well as the germs of a new industrial capitalist bourgeoisie. Russia was somewhat more industrialized than China, and therefore the Russian Revolution was carried out in the name of the working class, whereas the Chinese version was a peasants' revolution.

There has followed a kind of socialist imperialism. The countries of Eastern Europe have become socialist under the influence, and partly under the domination, of the USSR. North Korea and North Vietnam, adjacent to China, have undergone a similar development. In both cases this has to do with the Cold War: the main part of Western Europe became allied to the United States in NATO in 1949, and South Korea and South Vietnam were supported by the United States in two violent wars.

Economic and social instability has often been accompanied by political instability. Between the first and second world wars dictatorships were established, first in Italy and then in Germany. In the latter case, Hitler's takeover was facilitated partly by the conditions of the peace treaty after World War I and partly by the great depression of the 1930s. This takeover, again, contributed much to the tensions leading to World War II.

In the years since 1945 a large number of military coups have taken place in various parts of the world. Both the causes and the effects have varied from case to case, and there can be no question of drawing up their balance sheet here. There is, however, one thing about these events that gives food for thought, and that is that most of them have taken place in Africa and in Latin America. This can be taken as an indication of a fairly widespread instability in the societies of these two continents.

In some of the previous sections I have drawn attention to other similarieies between Africa and Latin America, which as I have said have the characteristics of dual societies to a larger extent than other parts of the world. They are therefore, socially unbalanced, and in particular have no strong and multifarious middle class to serve as a binding link between the extremes of a small elite or upper class and a great majority of poor people.

This is understandable in the case of Africa, where the full impact of contacts with modern HICs came late. It is more thought-provoking, however, that Latin America still has much of the same features after a long period of independence. It seems to confirm what I have said in the third section of this chapter, that Latin American countries have kept much of the former social structure of the two European countries by which they were colonized. To this was added a domination of the original Indian population by a European minority, and though races have been mixed to a large extent, there is still a correlation between color and economic and social status.

NOTES

1. Felix Paukert, "Income Distribution at Different Levels of Development: A survey of Evidence," *International Labour Review* 108, nos. 2 and 3, pp. 97-125.

2. See John Kenneth Galbraith, *A China Passage*, (Boston: Houghton Mifflin, 1973), p. 127.

3. United Nations, *1970 Report on the World Social Situation* (New York: the UN, 1917).

4. Ibid., p. 185.

5. Ibid., p. vii.

6. Ibid., p. 185.

7. Ibid., p. 5.

8. Ibid., p. 168.

9. Mariano Pison-Salas, *The Fate of the Indians, in Latin America Yesterday and Today* (New York: Bantam Books, 1973), p. 55.

10. Basil Davidson, *The Africans* (London: Penguin Books, 1973), p. 67.

11. UNESCO, *Cultural Patterns and Technical Change* (New York: Mentor Books, 1955), p. 188.

12. Ibid.

13. V. Gordon Childe, *What Happened in History* (rev. ed., Harmondsworth, England, 1972), p. 152.

CHAPTER

6

POPULATION DEVELOPMENT

There is a growing literature about population problems, and discussion of population development has been lively during the last few years. What I intend to do in this chapter is to consider population development as an integral part of the development process as a whole. What follows will therefore be closely related to other chapters in this book. How does social change influence population development, and how does population development influence social change?

We may begin by a look at *motivation*. The human desire to improve the situation for self, family, or nation makes it desirable to work for better nutrition, housing, and health services; progress in these fields tends to reduce the risk of early death. Reduced mortality rates and increased expectation of life have continued slowly over a long period in the countries that have been continuously in "the main stream of human progress" referred to in Chapter 3.

Human motivation also influences the number of births. There can be no doubt that since far back in history most people have had some vague ideas about the order of magnitude, rather than the exact number, of family that was most desirable. Deliberate measures to reduce the number of children surviving by, say, leaving some of them to die of exposure, are known from various societies. What is new in our time is only that techniques are more sophisticated in this field, as in so many others, and that deliberate policies of family planning are pursued by many governments. Expressed in another way this means that man want to control his destiny in various respects, including the circumstances that influence death and procreation. In this way we get the so-called demographic transition. Societies move from a situation with high death rates and high birth rates, similar to that of many kinds of animals, towards a new situation that is under deliberate human control to the extent considered possible.

There are two more general remarks that I find it necessary to make at this point. One is that the influence of governments is limited in this field. They can encourage or discourage family planning, but the real decision-makers are the individual couples, and no policy can be effective without influencing their motivation. In this respect there is no difference between socialist countries and other countries.

The other important remark to make is that there is probably no single factor that has more influence on the birth rate, than the death rate. I do not think that this is generally taken into account to the extent that it deserves. Of course the demographic transition means that falling death rates are followed by falling birth rates, but the time lag may be long, and therefore the causation is not always easily seen. It is nevertheless something fundamental: it is inconceivable that death rates could go on falling through many generations without birth rates following in their wake.

Infant mortality is particularly important in this respect. If many children die as babies or in their first years, parents will go on having extra children so that at least some will grow up. But if they become confident that children are now surviving to a much larger extent than before, they will gradually reduce procreation even if they have never heard about family planning.

There are a number of other factors that influence birth rates. Dudley Kirk has found a clear correlation between social development in seven fields and falling birth rates. The seven fields are urbanization, growth in nonagricultural employment, literacy, the number of telephones, the number of hospital beds, newspaper circulation, and female life expectancy. He admits, however, that this is a statistical measure of association, rather than a direct causal explanation,[1] and he does not discuss how the seven social indicators are correlated with death rates. In actual fact, what they signify is that in general the conditions of life are improving; this may well have influenced birth rates more through a reduction of death rates than directly. This is not to say that the social standard is of minor importance—on the contrary; but in considering its influence one should look at death rates as well as birth rates. A picture of development in this field from 1960 to 1970 is shown in Table 6.1.

It is remarkable that death rates have gone up in five of the seven income groups. In Groups 2 and 3 this probably has to do with the increasing life expectancy. In Group 2 there are now relatively many old people, as shown in Table 6.3. In the three lowest income groups, and in particular in Group 7, the situation is very different, since there are fewer old people in the poor countries. One must look for other causes to explain the high death rate.

Admittedly, only a relatively small part of the 78 countries belonging to Groups 5 through 7 are covered by the table. It is, however, worth noting that there is at least no fall in overall mortality in any of these groups, although infant mortality has gone down. The sharp rise in the death rate for Group 7 is because of deterioration in India, where nutrition has also become poorer, as mentioned in the fourth section of Chapter 5.

There is reason to believe that adverse developments in nutrition and housing are at least part of the explanation of the high and rising death rates. It was stressed in the fourth and fifth sections of Chapter 5 that there had been a deterioration in these fields for the poorer part of the population in low income countries; Group 5 represents the highest degree of inequality of incomes. (See Table 5.5.) That infant mortality was still high in 1970 seems to

TABLE 6.1

Birth Rates and Death Rates

Group	Number of Countries	Population 1967 (millions)	Birth Rate[a] 1960	Birth Rate[a] 1970	Death Rate[a] 1960	Death Rate[a] 1970	Infant Mortality[b] 1960	Infant Mortality[b] 1970	Natural Increase 1960	Natural Increase 1970
1	9	306.6	22.2	17.8	9.7	9.5	25.3	18.5	12.5	8.3
2	11	238.4	18.1	15.6	10.5	11.2	32.0	22.6	7.6	4.4
3	10	442.1	22.8	18.6	7.5	8.1	39.2	26.2	15.3	10.5
4	13	140.4	32.0	27.5	9.9	8.7	67.9	51.4	22.1	18.8
5	13	78.2	43.0	45.0	12.4	13.3	91.5	75.2	30.6	31.7
6	8	138.8	37.3	42.3	12.2	13.4	84.6	69.3	25.1	28.9
7	2	515.8	39.3	42.9	11.2	16.8	146.8	138.8	28.0	26.1
Total	66	1,860.3	29.3	28.3	10.0	11.8	73.5	62.8	19.3	16.5

[a]Per 1000 inhabitants.
[b]Per 1000 born, died before reaching 1 year.
Source: *UN Demographic Yearbook 1961 and 1970* (New York: United Nations).

support the view that a large part of the population was still living under miserable social conditions.

Concerning birth rates, the table shows an increase during the 1960s in Groups 5 through 7, the same groups that had high and rising death rates. There is no doubt that there is a connection between these two phenomena: as long as death rates are high there is no motivation for a reduction in the level of procreation, and rising death rates may even work in the opposite direction, although this is doubtful, since infant mortality has fallen somewhat. What can be said about these relationships is probably that infant mortality rates must go down over a rather long period and stay at a considerably lower level before people will become confident that children are now really surviving in a new way.

The situation concerning mortality in the three lowest income groups could therefore not be expected to lead to lower birth rates.* That birth rates have not only remained high, but have shown an upward trend, may be explained by the availability of modern health services on an increasing scale; this increases the chances for successful delivery and thus contributes to a higher number of live births, and may also be the main cause of the reduction in the infant mortality rates in the poor countries.

Birth rates reached their highest level in Group 5, which therefore showed the highest rate of natural increase. If we move further upwards in the table we find a very important reduction in birth rates, while death rates do not change nearly so much, partly because there are many old people in the rich countries. It is therefore in the range of medium income countries that the demographic transition really gets underway. Here we find yet another example showing that this is the category of countries in which social change takes place the fastest.

Group 1, however, shows higher birth rates than Group 2. The explanation of that is found in Table 6.2, where the various regions are compared. North America and Oceania have had substantially higher birth rates than Europe, though the difference was decreasing during the 1960s. This is an argument against the view sometimes held that higher incomes as a general rule lead to lower birth rates; there are other arguments against this view. That it does not apply to the lowest income groups is seen clearly from Table 6.1. It can be added that during the Great Depression in the 1930s, birth rates in a number of industrialized countries were low compared with their previous and later levels.

It has sometimes been assumed, other things being equal, that population growth is faster is sparsely populated countries than where there is already a greater concentration of people. Other things are seldom equal, however, and therefore no "law" can be demonstrated regarding this possible difference. At any rate it is probably now less important than the general trend towards low birth rates in Western countries with a high degree of urbanization. The

---

*It would have been desirable to study fertility as measured by the numbers of births compared with the numbers of women in certain age groups. Information about this is only available for rather few countries; the results, where they exist, are similar to those based on crude birth rates.[2]

TABLE 6.2

Birth Rates and Death Rates, by Categories and Regions

	Number of Countries	Population 1967 (millions)	Birth Rate[a] 1960	Birth Rate[a] 1970	Death Rate[a] 1960	Death Rate[a] 1970	Infant Mortality[b] 1960	Infant Mortality[b] 1970	Natural Increase 1960	Natural Increase 1970
HICs	18	539.6	20.3	16.7	10.1	10.2	28.2	20.2	10.2	6.5
North America and Oceania	4	234.1	23.7	18.3	9.3	9.2	25.4	19.6	14.4	9.1
Europe	14	305.5	17.7	15.5	10.7	11.0	30.2	20.7	7.0	4.5
MICs	36	660.7	27.1	23.6	8.5	8.8	51.5	37.4	18.6	14.8
Japan	1	99.9	17.2	18.9	7.6	6.9	30.7	13.1	9.6	12.0
USSR	1	235.5	24.9	17.5	7.1	8.2	35.0	24.4	17.8	9.3
Latin America	17	149.2	39.1	37.6	10.9	10.0	80.6	65.6	28.2	27.6
Other MICs	17	176.1	25.5	22.5	9.1	9.1	60.7	44.6	16.4	13.4
LICs	10	654.6	38.8	42.7	11.4	16.1	133.4	123.9	27.4	26.6
Asia	6	613.6	38.3	42.6	10.7	15.9	131.6	124.4	27.6	26.7
Africa	4	41.0	46.8	45.2	22.0	18.6	161.0	116.4	24.8	26.6
Total	64	1,854.9	29.3	28.3	10.0	11.8	73.6	63.0	19.3	16.5

Source: UN Demographic Yearbook 1961 and 1970 (New York: United Nations).

tendency in that direction has been strengthened by the fact that many married women are now seeking work on the labor market. It is also furthered by more liberal legislation concerning abortion and by new techniques of contraception. Population growth is now very slow in some European countries.

Among the MICs, the Latin American countries have conspicuously high birth rates, and little change has occured during the decade. This may have something to do with the fact that the influence of the Roman Catholic church has been strong in Latin America, although it does not seem that the official attitude of the Pope towards birth control has influenced the behavior of people strongly during the last few years. It is interesting to note that birth rates in European countries that are predominately Roman Catholic are much lower than in Latin America. In 1970 the birth rate was 19.8 in Spain, 18 in Portugal, and only 16.8 in Italy.

In fact, the Latin American experience seems to confirm what has been said above about the relationship between birth rates and death rates, and especially infant mortality rates. It will be noted that infant mortality was much higher in Latin American countries than in other MICs that in some respects have similar development indicators. The difference was even slightly greater in 1970 than in 1960, and the main explanation is no doubt to be found in the social structure of Latin America referred to in Chapter 5.

Among the LICs, both death rates and birth rates are slightly higher in Africa than in Asia. Only a small part of the African continent is represented in Table 6.2, however, and as far as Asia is concerned such important countries as China, Indonesia, and Pakistan are left out because only part of the figures were available. Birth rates and death rates were, however, available for these countries for the year 1970, and it may be of interest to compare them with the corresponding rates for India:

	Birth Rate	Death Rate
China	33.1	15.3
India	42.8	16.7
Pakistan	50.9	18.4
Indonesia	48.3	19.4

These figures show that the demographic transition has advanced considerably further in China than in the other three countries, and a little further in India than in Pakistan and Indonesia. It can therefore be expected that future population growth will be considerably slower in China than in the big countries of South and Southeast Asia.

Table 6.2 gives the general impression that high income countries are entering a period of very slow population growth; the underlying trend in that direction may be even stronger than indicated by the table. There was in several countries a "baby boom" immediately after World War II; this would normally lead to a new baby boom 20 to 25 years later, or around the year 1970, but there are no clear signs of that happening. I have been able to compare birth rates for 1967 and 1971 for fourteen of the HICs, and the weighed average was as follows:

	1967	1971
Group 1	17.7	17.3
Group 2	17.5	15.3

Maybe there was a slight indication of the boom in 1967, but that is uncertain.

Concerning MICs, the figures indicate a trend towards substantially lower rates of population growth in the years ahead, perhaps with the exception of Latin America. The very low death rate for Japan may well begin to increase, as it has done in Europe, when the number of old people becomes more important.

For the LICs there is still a long way to go before a marked slowing down can be expected. Death rates and in particular infant mortality rates must show a considerable, sustained decline before birth rates are likely to go down in an important way.

One of the consequences of different patterns of population development is that the age composition of the population changes in ways that vary rather much from one group of countries to another. This is shown in Table 6.3. As could be expected there are relatively many old people in the richer countries and relatively few in the poorer ones. Unfortunately, few of the poorest countries are covered by the table, but Groups 5 and 6 represent a rather large percentage of their total population, and the figures for the three lowest income groups show a considerable degree of regularity.

The most important feature of the situation as depicted by the table is that in Groups 5 through 7 the number of children 14 years or less is very high in proportion to the number of people at working age, 15-64 years, while the opposite is true of Groups 1 through 3. Group 4 stands in between. Two conclusions can be drawn.

The first is that what one might call the working population will be growing slowly in the period 1971-85 in the richer countries, while its growth will be much faster in the poorer countries. This makes it likely that there will continue to be a labor shortage in the former countries and a labor abundance in the latter. Combined with a rising standard of education in MICs and LICs, such a development should facilitate a further transfer of labor intensive production processes to low-wage countries.

The other conclusion to be drawn from the high proportion of children in the population of the poorer countries is that the number of young people in these countries will grow rapidly in the next couple of decades, and probably more than from 1960 to 1970, since birth rates were high in 1970. More specifically, one can be sure that there will be many women in the childbearing age groups.

It follows that birth rates will remain high even if the average fertility begins to go down rather soon. There may be fewer children born per family, but there will be many families of which the parents are young. This, then, confirms the impression given by Tables 6.1 and 6.2 that population growth rates will remain high in the present LICs for a fairly long time to come. In this, as in many other respects, the gap between MICs and LICs is therefore likely to widen in the next two or three decades.

TABLE 6.3

Population, by Age Groups

Group	Number of Countries	Population 1967 (millions)	14 or less 1960	14 or less 1970	Percent of Total 15-64 1960	15-64 1970	65 or more 1960	65 or more 1970
1	9	234.1	29.9	27.5	60.4	62.1	9.7	10.4
2	11	305.5	24.1	24.7	65.5	63.5	10.4	11.8
3	10	442.1	31.5	28.9	62.2	63.5	6.3	7.6
4	10	134.4	34.7	35.6	59.5	58.0	5.8	6.4
5	9	214.5	44.4	45.9	51.8	50.5	3.8	3.7
6	4	291.4	44.7	44.6	52.1	52.4	3.2	3.0
7	4	523.9	41.7	41.6	55.2	55.2	3.1	3.2
Total	57	2,145.9	34.4	34.0	59.3	59.2	6.3	6.8

Source: UN Demographic Yearbook 1970 (New York: United Nations).

NOTES

1. Dudley Kirk, "A New Demographic Transition?" *Rapid Population Growth*, vol. II (Baltimore: Johns Hopkins Press, 1971).

2. Ibid., p. 145.

INTERNATIONAL RELATIONS

In the present phase of history nearly all parts of the world are organized as national states. The economic and political relations between these states are therefore important factors in the present process of development. It is the purpose of this chapter to examine these relationships in connection with the economic and social development already discussed.

TRADE

It is often said that the so-called developing countries have been losing ground in international trade, since their exports represent a declining percentage of world exports and their terms of trade have deteriorated. It will appear from the following analysis that this is a misleading statement. It is necessary to distinguish between more than two categories of countries and also between the various parts of the flow of trade in order to get a realistic picture of the actual development.

The terms of trade of course depend on the pattern of trade of each individual country. In the statistics of the General Agreement on Tariffs and Trade (GATT), the unit values in world exports of the three major categories of goods traded are calculated as follows for the year 1969 (1960 = 100):[1]

Agricultural products	104
Minerals	115
Manufactures	108
Total	108

It is customary to think of developing countries as exporting agricultural products and minerals and importing manufactures. Even if this were a true picture of reality the terms of trade would depend on the composition of the exports. In any case the price movements are modest for a nine-year period, and since in practice manufactures and primary products appear together in both the exports and imports of all countries, changes in the terms of trade cannot have been important in the decade considered here. The same is true of price movements in general. Therefore one can study trade as measured in current prices. In Table 7.1 this is done for the usual seven income groups of countries.

Since manufactured products are increasingly dominating international trade I have extracted the figures in Table 7.2 regarding the exports of manufactures from Table 7.1. Manufactures are playing an increasing role in the exports of all seven groups, and in none of them were they unimportant in 1969. It is also worth noting that the relative increase in the exports of manufactures was greater in Groups 3, 5, and 6 than it was in the two groups of HICs. It would also have been greater in Group 4 than in Group 2, had not the latter been enhanced by the two free-trade arrangements in Europe, the EEC and EFTA, which made trade between European countries free to a large extent during the period under consideration.

We see here the effects of a fundamental trend that has been at work for at least the last fifteen years. There is a labor shortage in the rich countries because the rapid expansion of the existing knowledge makes so many new things technically feasible that demand for labor increases faster than supply.

Therefore, in more and more cases labor intensive production processes are undertaken in countries with lower wage levels, and the products are then exported to the richer countries. The multinational corporations play an important role in this process, which is one of the ways of counteracting the structural unemployment discussed in the second section of Chapter 5.

A more complete picture of the trade flows is given in Table 7.2, where it has been possible to include all the socialist countries in Europe and Asia, while only the USSR is included in Table 7.1.

If in this table the total exports in 1960 are given the value 100, we get the following figures for 1969 for the three main categories of countries:

HICs	217
MICs	269
LICs	143

In this as in other fields the medium income countries have had a faster growth than the high income and low income countries. The difference would have been even greater, had not the free-trade arrangements in Europe mentioned above furthered intra-European trade substantially in the period considered.

As already mentioned the growth has been particularly fast concerning exports of manufacturers. If we extract the relevant figures in the same way we did for Table 7.1 we get the picture shown in Table 7.4.

The progress of Japanese exports is remarkable. Japan is now dependent almost exclusively on exports of manufactures. There has of course at the same time been a substantial increase in the imports of raw materials, but Japan's own consumption of manufactured goods has also largely been made possible

TABLE 7.1

International Trade, 1960 and 1969[a]
(billions of dollars)

Group	Food, SITC[c] 0-1 + 4				Raw Materials[b] SITC[c] 2-3				Manufactures, SITC[c] 5-9				Total Trade			
	Imports		Exports		Imports		Exports		Imports		Exports		Imports		Exports	
	1960	1969	1960	1969	1960	1969	1960	1969	1960	1969	1960	1969	1960	1969	1960	1969
1	5.9	9.7	6.9	11.3	10.1	14.8	8.2	13.9	19.9	63.4	27.2	60.4	35.9	87.9	42.3	85.6
2	8.8	11.1	2.2	5.6	12.2	20.0	3.9	6.5	17.2	54.7	28.5	70.0	38.2	85.8	34.6	82.1
3	1.5	4.0	2.2	3.5	4.6	10.3	2.6	6.8	6.7	17.8	3.4	22.8	12.8	32.1	8.2	33.1
4	1.0	1.6	1.5	2.0	1.8	2.2	2.3	2.6	6.0	10.9	2.7	6.5	8.8	14.7	6.5	11.1
5	0.3	0.5	2.4	3.5	0.7	1.0	0.7	1.4	2.8	5.1	0.2	1.4	3.8	6.6	13.3	6.3
6	0.7	1.2	1.2	1.9	0.4	1.1	1.9	2.2	2.6	5.3	0.3	1.2	3.7	7.6	3.4	5.3
7	0.6	0.7	0.9	1.1	0.6	0.6	0.9	1.4	2.6	2.7	0.7	1.2	3.8	4.0	2.5	3.7
Total	18.8	28.8	17.3	28.9	30.4	50.0	20.5	34.8	57.8	159.9	63.0	163.5	107.0	238.7	100.8	227.2

[a]Imports C.I.F., exports F.O.B.
[b]Including fuels.
[c]Standard International Trade Classification.

Note: Of the socialist countries only the USSR is included, while in Table 7.2 the socialist countries of Europe and Asia are also covered.

Sources: United Nations, *Yearbook of International Trade Statistics 1969,* (New York: the UN, 1969); and (for the USSR) United Nations, *Handbook of International Trade and Developments Statistics 1972* (New York: the UN, 1972).

TABLE 7.2

Exports of Manufactured Goods

Group	Manufactures as Percent of Total Exports		Exports of Manufactures
	1960	1969	1969 (1960=100)
1	64.5	70.6	222
2	82.4	85.3	246
3	41.5	68.9	671
4	41.5	58.6	241
5	15.0	22.2	700
6	8.0	22.7	400
7	28.0	32.4	171
Average	62.5	72.0	260

Source: Compiled by the author from figures in Table 7.1.

through imports. Japan confirms the general observation that the more countries industrialize the more they trade with one another in products of industry as a result of increasing specialization.

Another interesting detail to be noted is the low level of exports of manufactures from Latin America; it is even lower than the relative level for LICs in Asia. Here again we find a certain similarity between Latin America and Africa. The level has, however, been increasing rather fast as far as Latin America is concerned, probably because economic development in Latin America has been speeding up in recent years.

As will be seen from the second footnote to Table 7.4, the increase in the industrial exports of nonsocialist Asian countries has been fairly rapid. This is of some importance because Asia is short of land and many people will be released from agriculture in the decades to come. The transfer of labor intensive industrial production to low-wage countries mentioned above is therefore one of Asia's possibilities.

Going back to Table 7.3, it is worth noting that the trade in primary products (food and raw materials) is far from being a one-way traffic from "developing" to "developed" countries, as one may have been brought to believe by reading some parts of the literature about development. True, the HICs are the largest importers of food and raw materials, but they are also the largest exporters, and the MICs represented in the table are net importers of raw materials.

It must be added that although Table 7.3 is relatively complete, covering about 90 percent of world exports, something important is lacking, since figures were not available for such leading oil-exporting countries as Algeria, Iran, Iraq, and Saudi Arabia. It must also be remembered that Kuwait and a few other oil

TABLE 7.3

International Trade, by Categories and Regions, 1960 and 1969
(billions of dollars)

	Number of Countries	Population 1967 (millions)	Food, SITC* 0-1 + 4				Raw Materials, SITC* 2-3				Manufactures, SITC* 5-9				Total Trade			
			Imports		Exports		Imports		Exports		Imports		Exports		Imports		Exports	
			1960	1969	1960	1969	1960	1969	1960	1969	1960	1969	1960	1969	1960	1969	1960	1969
HICs	16	508.2	14.6	20.7	9.0	16.7	22.2	34.6	12.1	20.4	36.8	117.1	55.6	129.7	73.6	172.4	76.7	166.8
North America and Oceania	4	234.1	3.8	5.8	5.0	7.5	5.9	8.3	7.0	10.9	12.7	39.2	17.5	37.5	22.4	53.3	29.5	55.9
Europe	12	274.1	10.8	14.9	4.0	9.2	16.3	26.3	5.1	9.5	24.1	77.9	38.1	92.2	51.2	119.1	47.2	110.0
MICs	36	758.7	4.2	8.1	7.2	11.2	9.4	16.6	7.0	12.5	19.4	46.1	11.2	42.6	33.0	70.8	25.4	66.3
Japan	1	99.9	0.6	2.1	0.3	0.6	2.9	8.4	0.1	0.3	1.0	4.4	0.4	15.1	4.5	14.9	0.8	16.0
USSR	1	235.5	0.7	1.3	0.8	1.2	1.0	0.9	1.9	3.5	3.6	9.3	2.8	6.9	5.3	11.5	5.5	11.6
Latin America	14	206.4	0.6	1.0	3.1	4.6	1.1	1.5	1.4	2.2	4.4	5.9	0.7	2.1	6.1	8.4	5.2	8.9
Other MICs	20	216.9	2.3	3.7	3.0	4.8	4.4	5.8	3.6	6.5	10.4	26.5	7.3	18.5	17.1	36.0	13.9	29.8
LICs	31	1,690.6	1.4	2.3	2.8	3.8	1.5	2.1	3.3	4.0	6.7	9.7	1.9	3.5	9.6	14.1	8.0	11.3
Asia	10	1,501.6	1.0	1.7	2.1	2.4	1.3	1.7	2.2	2.3	4.9	7.1	1.7	3.1	7.2	10.5	6.0	7.8
Africa	21	189.0	0.4	0.6	0.7	1.4	0.2	0.4	1.1	1.7	1.8	2.6	0.2	0.4	2.4	3.6	2.0	3.5
Total	83	2,957.5	20.2	31.1	19.0	31.7	33.1	53.3	22.4	36.9	62.9	172.9	68.7	175.8	116.2	257.3	110.1	244.4

*Standard International Trade Classification.

Sources: United Nations, Yearbook of International Trade Statistics 1969 (New York: the UN, 1969); and (for the USSR) United Nations, Handbook of International Trade and Development Statistics 1972 (New York: the UN, 1972).

TABLE 7.4

**Exports of Manufactured Goods, by
Categories and Regions, 1960 and 1969**

	Manufactures as Percent of Total Exports		Exports of Manufactures
	1960	1969	1969 (1960=100)
HICs	72.5	77.8	233
North America and Oceania	59.3	67.1	214
Europe	80.7	83.1	242
MICs	44.9	64.3	380
Japan	50.0	94.4	3750
USSR	50.9	59.5	246
Latin America	13.5	23.6	300
Other MICs	52.5	62.1	253[a]
LICs	23.8	31.0	184
Asia	28.3	39.7	182[b]
Africa	10.0	11.4	200
Total	62.4	71.9	256

[a]Socialist countries   243
  Other countries   274
[b]Socialist countries   122
  Other countries   250

Source: United Nations, *Yearbook of International Trade Statistics 1969* (New York: the UN, 1969); and (for the USSR) United Nations, *Handbook of International Trade and Development Statistics 1972* (New York: United Nations, 1972).

exporters have less than one million inhabitants, and therefore are not included in any of the tables in this book. The inclusion of these countries would have increased the export figures for "Other MICs" in a remarkable way.

I think this is the place for a remark about primary products that it is essential to make. The important division-line in this field is not between "developed" and "developing" countries, but between countries that are rich in certain natural resources and countries that are not. The table shows that the region "North America and Oceania" is a net exporter of both food and raw materials, while Europe (that is, Western Europe) is the world's largest net importer of both.

We may now be entering a new phase in the use of oil and certain raw materials. For many years it has been clear to careful observers that the only way to get higher prices for certain commodities is for the main exporters to get together. This is what the oil exporting countries have been doing since the beginning of the 1970s, and quite particularly since the fall of 1973. At the same time Morocco has increased the price of phosphate rock, of which she is the main exporter. Something similar may happen to a few other raw materials.

Such a development would mean a great advantage for some MICs and LICs and a disadvantage for others. By early 1974 it was beginning to have important consequences for the balance of payments of many countries and for the world's capital markets. More will be said about this in the next section and in Chapter 9.

The industrial development of MICs and LICs will increase their own demand for both materials and energy very much in the years to come. For some of them this will mean that they will have rather limited quantities of raw materials left for export even if the demand from HICs goes on increasing. Industrial production is growing faster in most regions of so-called developing countries than in the old industrialized countries, as seen in Table 7.5.

Apart from the industial weakness of Latin America, this table confirms the view expressed above that the demand for raw materials in MICs and LICs is likely to rise faster than in HICs, which on their part will have a labor shortage. It is therefore likely that the trade pattern of MICs in the next few decades will be closer to that of HICs, with more exporting of manufactures and less of raw materials. For LICs this development may be slower.

The term "food" in Table 7.3 covers food in the narrower sense as well as beverages (wine, coffee, tea, cocoa) and tobacco. Some of these products are of great importance as earners of foreign exchange for a number of tropical and subtropical MICs and LICs. The tables therefore do not represent a balance sheet for food as such. The problems concerning food supply and demand will

TABLE 7.5

**Average annual Rate of Growth of Manufacturing Output, 1960-67
(percent)**

Area	Rate of Growth
Industrialized countries	5.6
Developing countries	7.3
Southern Europe	10.1
Latin America	5.5
Middle East	10.8
East Asia	7.5
South Asia	6.9
Africa	6.0

Source: Lester B. Pearson, *Partners in Development,* (New York: Praeger Publishers, 1969), p. 36.

be dealt with in Chapter 9 as one of the most important questions of the future. It is, however, of interest at this point to give an indication of some essential features of the food market. This is done in Table 7.6, which gives a picture of world trade and production for all cereals taken together. Cereals are the most important element of food consumption, partly directly, and partly indirectly as feeding stuff for domestic animals. They are also the most important element in food trade.

The second largest item in the food trade is meat. In this case it may suffice to indicate the size of net exports in 1967 for the main areas of the world, in millions of tons. (Imports are expressed as negatives.)[2]

Europe	-1.2
USSR	+0.1
North & Central America	-0.2
South America	+0.6
Asia	-0.1
Africa	0.0
Oceania	+0.8

The dominant importer is Europe, and the main exporters are Australia, New Zealand, Argentina, and Uruguay.

TABLE 7.6

Trade and Production of All Cereals, 1967
(millions of tons)

	Imports	Exports	Net Exports	Production
HICs	39.0	71.4	+32.4	361.5
North America and Oceania	1.2	59.6	+58.4	246.3
Europe	37.8	11.8	-26.0	115.2
MICs	36.3	25.3	-11.0	352.7
Japan	12.0	0.1	-11.9	21.0
USSR	2.9	6.8	+ 3.9	141.3
Latin America	7.1	10.0	+ 2.9	62.7
Other MICs	14.3	8.4	- 5.9	127.7
LICs	25.5	6.4	-19.1	421.6
Asia	20.3	5.2	-15.1	378.1
Africa	5.2	1.2	- 4.0	43.5
Total	100.8	103.1	+ 2.3	1,135.8

Source: *FAO Trade Yearbook 1971* (Rome: Food and Agricultural Organization).

Taken together, this information about food trade shows that by far the largest net exporter is the region including North America and Oceania. The largest importer is Europe, followed by Asia, including Japan. Latin America is an important net exporter of meat. As regards the USSR the situation fluctuates from one year to another, as it also does for other large continental areas like India and Africa.

In this important field much will depend on the future development of population and purchasing power on the one hand and of productive capacity on the other. It will therefore be a major subject of Chapter 9.

OTHER ECONOMIC TRANSACTIONS

Non-trade transactions fall into two broad categories: the first is services, which are sometimes also called invisible trade because they do not appear in the trade statistics; the other is movements of three of the factors of production from one country to another.

Services

Into this category come transport services by land, sea, and air; insurance; tourism; and various minor items. They represent balance-of-payments income for one country and expenditure for another.

The most important, no doubt, is maritime transport, because a very large part of the goods traded between countries is transported by sea. In principle the trade statistics quoted in the first section 6 of this chapter include transport costs in the figures for imports but not in those for exports. The reason is that when goods are sent from one country to another, freights are income that accrues to the country owning the ship in question, whether it be the importer, the exporter, or a third country. The importing country must of course pay the full price, including transport costs.

It would, therefore, be of interest to know which countries are earning the incomes represented by transport costs. In the absence of such information, the distribution of the world's merchant fleet may give a rough indication of transport income distribution. In Table 7.7 the size of the fleets of the various groups of countries is compared with the size of the imports in 1969 of the same groups, as shown in Table 7.1.

It should be added that the following three countries are not included in the table because the fleets registered in them largely belong to other countries utilizing the advantages of "flags of convenience." Their registered fleets in 1969 amounted to the following (millions Gross Register Tons):

Liberia	33.3
Panama	5.6
Cyprus	1.1

TABLE 7.7

Imports and Sizes of Merchant Fleets

Group	Imports 1969 (billions of dollars)	Merchant fleet 1970 (millions Gross Register Tons)
1	87.9	52.9
2	85.8	50.5
3	32.1	61.8
4	14.7	4.0
5	6.6	3.7
6	7.6	2.3
7	4.0	3.9
Total	238.7	179.1

Sources: OECD, *Maritime Transport 1971* (Paris: OECD, 1971); United Nations, *Yearbook of International Trade Statistics 1969,* and (for the USSR) United Nations, *Handbook of International Trade and Developments Statistics 1972.*

It can be taken for granted that these ships almost exclusively belong to countries in Groups 1, 2, and 3 (including Greece). This being so, the figures, imperfect as they are, can generally be said to indicate that countries in Groups 1 through 3 are net earners in the field of maritime transport, while countries in Groups 4 through 7 earn less freight than they pay for their imports. Assuming that ships registered in Liberia, Panama, and Cyprus belong to owners in countries in Groups 1 through 3, these countries own some 94 percent of the total merchant fleet, while their imports represent about 86 percent of the total. Countries in Groups 4 through 7 own only about 6 percent of the total fleet, while their imports are some 14 percent of the total. What is said about maritime transport no doubt also applies to air transport and to the insurance of the goods transported.

It can be seen from Table 7.7 that Group 3 has a remarkably strong position compared with the size of its imports. This is mainly due to the fact that Japan and Greece, which belong to this group, have particularly large fleets in relation to the size of their economies.

Until recently international tourism has mainly consisted of people going from one high income country to another, but by the end of the 1960s a number of MICs had begun to attract tourists on a rather large scale, particularly in the Mediterranean area. Also, a few LICs are beginning to go into this kind of service, since modern technology has made hotel accommodation and air transport so comfortable that people from the temperate zone find it relatively easy to spend some time in tropical countries, about which they now know more and more because of the modern means of communication. It should be added that often the hotels in question are at least partly owned by corporations in the rich countries. Only part of the incomes created will therefore accrue to people in the tropical countries visited.

Factors of Production

Three of the four factors of production, namely labor, capital, and knowledge, can be moved, and their movements from one country to another have become important elements of the development process. This is one of the means by which the evolution of various national societies makes them more and more interdependent.

It is, therefore, worthwhile to study the causes and effects of the movements of these factors as seen in this context. Publicly available information about them is rather limited, and the following considerations do not pretend to be more than a general presentation of the main problems involved.

Labor

Forced labor movements on a considerable scale have taken place in the past, the most well-known being the slave trade that moved African labor to the Americas. The economic background of this incredibly inhumane activity was of course labor shortages in the "importing" areas. If it is generally true, as argued in Chapter 25 that an increasing supply of one factor of production strengthens the demand for the others, it can perhaps be said that the enormous amounts of land the European emigrants found in North and South America tempted them to seize more labor for the exploitation of these rich natural resources. The large-scale voluntary migration of Europeans to North America towards the end of the 19th century is a further consequence of this abundance of land.

In recent years the flow of labor from Southern Europe and North Africa to Northern Europe is probably the most spectacular case; similar is the movement of workers from Mexico and Puerto Rico to the United States.

In general these are partly temporary movements to countries with higher incomes not too far away. Some countries can have movements both in and out; many Greek workers have gone to Germany while North African workers have gone to Greece. There are also examples of movements over rather long distances, such as from Portugal to the United States and from Pakistan to Europe.

Until now it has probably been true that the bulk of this movement has been from MICs to HICs, where wages are higher. Greater abundance of capital and knowledge in the rich countries has increased the demand for labor. For the labor exporting countries this means that remittances to the workers' families at home contribute to the positive side of the balance of payments, and as a rule it also means that unemployment is smaller than it would be without this migration.

It is too early to judge the social and political consequences of these movements of people. Much of course will depend on the extent to which the movements prove to be permanent. In Spain, for instance, the rapid economic development at home has caused a certain number of workers to come back from abroad. When there has been an economic recession in the labor importing countries, foreign workers have had to return to their own countries, sometimes on a rather important scale. However, in a country like Switzerland the number of foreign workers has now been high for many years, and a certain change in the composition of the Swiss community seems likely to result. This may in a modest way be a parallel to the building up of the United States in the 19th century.

One of the questions of the future is, therefore, whether large-scale movements of labor are likely to become a permanent or semipermanent feature of the development to come. More will be said about this in Chapter 9. The migration of scientists and technicians from poor countries to countries with higher incomes is treated below under "knowledge" because this "brain drain" seems primarily to be a movement of that factor of production.

Capital

There is, no doubt, a certain flight of capital from medium and low income countries to high income countries in which it is considered to be more safely invested. Since these capital movements to a large extent are illegal, little is of course known about their size. If there is one general conclusion that can be drawn about them it is probably that they are most likely to be important in nonsocialist MICs, at times when rapid transformation of society makes the political system unstable. In some Latin American societies the instability may instead be due to a lack of adaptation of the social and political structures to the concepts of democracy that are spreading in the present century. Capital flight means that there is a certain amount of capital belonging to nations of some MICs that may be repatriated if confidence in the political stability of their countries should increase.

In spite of this capital movement of unknown size towards richer countries, the general trend has been in the opposite direction. The total balance of trade and services has on the whole been negative for most of the poorer countries and positive for most of the richer ones, the deficits of the former being accounted for by capital exports from the latter. These capital exports have various forms. Private investments by firms in high income countries seem to have been most important in medium and low income countries having considerable resources of oil or raw materials. More generally, United States firms have invested in a number of Latin American countries, as well as in a few countries in East Asia, in which Japanese firms are also beginning to invest.

In the aid programs of industrialized countries, capital exports appear partly as grants and partly as loans. Often there is a grant element in the loans because they are free of interest or at rates of interest lower than the market rates. The grant element of loans, and grants themselves, declined from 59 percent in 1965 to 45 percent in 1969.[3] The publicly available information only permits a rather imperfect description of the capital transfers between countries. What follows is based on World Bank statistics.[4]

Gross investment compared with savings as a percentage of gross national product in various groups of countries has been as shown in Table 7.8. Roughly speaking, the Industrialized countries in this table include the countries we have been calling HICs, plus Japan. South Asia, Africa, and part of East Asia correspond to LICs, while the remaining groups are MICs.

It will be seen that capital exports amounting to 5 to 6 percent of the total GNP of the industrialized countries have permitted all the other groups to invest considerably more than their own savings. There can be no doubt that this is one of the reasons the economic development shown in Chapter 4 has been faster, in medium income countries especially, than has often been assumed.

Since part of the capital transfers has been in loans, another consequence has of course been an increasing debt burden on the part of the receiving countries. The World Bank Report gives information only about external public debts. For developing countries these have increased by 14 percent per year in the period 1960-69, including debts committed by undisbursed loans. Since there has been some price increase, the growth of the real burden has been somewhat slower. Still it has grown considerably faster, on the average, than the total GNP of the debtor countries.

It would be of interest to compare debt burden with economic capacity for the various groups of countries treated in this essay. This has been possible with 70 countries, of which Israel, belonging to Group 2, is hardly typical. The remaining 69 countries represent about 93 percent of the total public debt (disbursed loans only) of developing countries counted in the World Bank Report. As a percentage of the GNP of the debtor countries in each group, this debt at the end of 1970 was as follows:[5]

TABLE 7.8

Investment and Savings*
(percent of GNP)

	Investment		Savings	
	1961-65	1966-69	1961-65	1966-69
Industrialized countries	21.4	21.8	21.9	22.4
Developing countries	18.5	19.2	16.1	16.6
Southern Europe	24.4	23.9	21.1	20.7
Latin America	19.3	19.3	18.2	17.6
Middle East	19.0	19.4	14.3	14.6
East Asia	15.1	19.3	11.5	15.9
South Asia	16.3	15.6	14.1	13.0
Africa	15.7	17.4	12.6	15.9

*Socialist countries not included.

Source: World Banks, *Annual Report 1971,* Washington, D.C.

Group	Debt as Percentage of GNP
3	7.7
4	8.8
5	11.8
6	18.2
7	15.8

In Group 4, Chile had a particularly high percentage, namely 28.4. Similarly, the percentage for Indonesia, in Group 6, was 33.1. In Group 7, India had a rather low percentage, namely 13.6. Apart from India the group's percentage was 20. Therefore, it is perhaps justified to say that typically the percentage is higher, the lower the income level of the group. The differences are, however, not very pronounced, and it should be remembered that private investment, export credits, and some other private credits are not included.

Private capital is, however, an important factor in economic relations between countries, and its role is increasing. The 1973 report from the Development Assistance Committee of OECD (DAC) has a table showing the flow of financial resources from member countries of DAC to developing countries in the years from 1962 to 1972.[6] For the first and the last three years of this period the annual flow was as follows (in billions of dollars):

	Official Assistance	Direct Private Investment
1962-64	5.7	1.6
1970-72	7.8	3.9

To write about direct foreign investment is to write about multinational corporations, which represent a factor of growing importance in the movement towards a world economy that we are witnessing. These corporations are one of the most interesting results of the knowledge expansion of our time. As I described in Chapter 2, in contrast to the other factors of production, knowledge has an unlimited capacity. If a firm has developed a good product through its research work, the bigger the market it can supply the better, and therefore successful firms are growing beyond the frontiers of their home countries and establishing subsidiaries wherever there is a market. Modern means of communication, another product of the knowledge expansion, permit managing directors to follow and to steer their firms' activities in many countries. Fifty years ago the possibilities for that were much more limited; therefore the great expansion of the multinational corporations is coming only now.

These corporations are of course much more than an instrument for the transfer of capital: they also transfer technical and other knowledge, and they influence the patterns of production and employment in their home country as well as in the various host countries where they operate.

We are far from having reached a satisfactory level of understanding of the full impact of their activities, but a 1973 report from the United Nations contains some interesting information from which the following figures are extracted.[7] The report contains a survey of direct foreign investment, having its origin in the 16 member countries of DAC, which represent North America, Western Europe, Japan, and Australia, virtually the HICs. By the end of 1967 the distribution was as follows (in billions of dollars):

Country of origin		Region of investment	
United States	59.5	Industrialized countries	71.1
United Kingdom	17.5		
France	6.0	Developing countries	33.1
Switzerland	4.3	Latin America	18.4
Canada	3.7	Middle East	3.1
Western Germany	3.0	Asia	5.0
Other countries	10.2	Africa	6.6
Total	104.2		

For a long time the United Kingdom was the origin of foreign investment on a large scale in overseas countries. The United States came later into this business but is now dominating. During the last decade or so Western Germany and Japan have extended their investments rapidly. The bulk of the investment flow still runs between HICs, and there is no clear sign that this is changing. For U.S. corporations the main areas of operation have been Western Europe, Canada, and Latin America.

Concerning the regions described in the report as "developing countries," it is remarkable how small the investments are in Asia, since even apart from China it has more inhabitants than Africa and Latin America taken together. The investments in the Middle East have of course been attracted mainly by the oil resources of that region. In other areas investment was also originally made mainly for the exploitation of natural resources, but they are increasingly being directed towards manufacturing, attracted by cheap labor and growing markets.

From the figures concerning region of investment it seems evident that the relatively small industrial sectors of Latin America and Africa are dominated by foreign investment to a much higher degree than industry in Asia. This of course confirms the view expressed in other parts of this book that not only Africa but also Latin America are on the whole much more "dual" in their societies than Asia. The internal industrial development of Latin American societies has not been strong or broad enough to fill the vacuum created by the release of manpower from agriculture. Therefore the foreign firms are playing a part that is remarkable in view of the fact that Latin America became independent so long ago.

The impact of the activities of multinational corporations is very difficult to evaluate. One can measure the inflow of capital and the outflow of royalties, fees, and dividends but the net effects on production, employment, and exports and imports can be estimated at best with large margins of error.

The UN report contains some information about the royalties and fees paid by a few countries as a percentage of their GNP and their exports in the late 1960s:[8]

	Percent of GNP	Percent of Exports
Argentina	.72	7.9
Brazil	.26	3.4

Continued on next page

Continued from previous page

	Percent of GNP	Percent of Exports
Columbia	.50	5.3
Mexico	.76	15.9
Nigeria	.78	4.2
Sri Lanka	.51	2.9

What is not shown in these figures is how much GNP and exports have been increased by the activity of the multinational corporations. The exports of manufactures by Mexico, for instance, were much more important than those by the three South American countries. Imports have probably been reduced by the production of some of the foreign firms, but this cannot be seen from the statistics available.

Of a more general nature is the information contained in the UN report[9] about the inflow of foreign direct investment and the outflow of income on accumulated past investment in some selected developing countries. The figures for the year 1970 are as follows (in billions of dollars):

	Oil-producing Countries	Non-Oil-producing Countries
Inflow	0.3	1.3
Outflow	3.7	1.7

For the non-oil-producing countries an evaluation of these figures would only be possible if information were also available about the impact of the multinational coporations on imports, exports, investment, production, and employment in the countries in question. The only conclusion one can draw from the figures published in the report is that these enterprises represent an important element of society in some of the countries in which the multinational corporations operate.

The situation of the oil-producing countries is likely to change in a drastic way because of the recent increases of oil prices and also because the host countries have taken over a large part of the stock of foreign oil companies. More will be said about this in Chapter 9.

The same applies to multinational corporations in general. The discussion about these enterprises has often been value-laden; let it be said, therefore, that they have grown up as a natural and unavoidable consequence of the knowledge expansion of our time. There is no reason why the expansion of a productive institution should stop at the frontiers of the country in which it started. Their most lasting effect may be to tie national economies closer together and to transfer technology and production to poorer countries. In the meantime they are having a number of effects on the economies of the countries concerned, and the true effects are often obscure because the big corporations can concentrate much of their activities in countries where control is ineffective. There will therefore be important policy issues concerning multinational corporations in the years to come.

Knowledge

It is in the nature of knowledge to spread, and thanks to the modern means of communication, new knowledge produced by research or by practical experience tends to spread rapidly. There can hardly be any doubt that this movement of knowledge has contributed more than any other factor to the drawing of virtually all countries into the process of development that is characteristic of the years since World War II.

Transfer of knowledge between states takes place in many forms. To the extent that knowledge is published in books and periodicals or through the modern mass media, it is of course available everywhere at costs that are negligible, but the question is whether a certain country will have people who themselves have sufficient knowledge to select and absorb the kinds of information that can serve the needs of that country. This is one of the reasons why international transfer of knowledge is related to the standard of education in the knowledge-importing countries.

If knowledge is patented, the cost of importing it can be considerable, as mentioned above in connection with capital transfer through multinational corporations. There can even be indirect costs that are not easily detected; if a firm in, say, an LIC has to buy capital goods on intermediary products from an enterprise in an HIC, the prices quoted may contain an element that is in fact a payment for the knowledge embodied in the goods. The possession of such knowledge can give the supplier a quasi-monopolistic position. Negotiating partners are not equal if one of them is in a stronger position concerning relevant knowledge than the other; to be strongly dependent on foreign firms technologically can be a serious weakness for a country.

This is only one aspect of the complicated problems regarding the flow of knowledge between countries that are on greatly different levels in this respect. In the long run modern knowledge is bound to spread to all countries, but the interval can be very long in some cases. It can be a tedious task to steer the flow of knowledge and its absorption in the receiving countries. The emphasis should be on absorption. The crucial question is how to select for importation the knowledge that can be absorbed by the community in the most productive and harmonious way. A selection is needed because the absorptional capacity is limited and the choices made have both economic and cultural implications.

The future problems of an appropriate policy for the importation and absorption of knowledge will be discussed in Chapter 9. In this section I shall only make some analytical remarks about these processes as they have gone on in recent years.

The crucial factor has been the educational system of the receiving countries, one of the functions of which is, to be the instrument through which parts of the existing knowledge are channeled to various strata of society in the receiving country.

In this respect it has been of fatal importance that most LICs and many MICs have been colonies of European countries until recently and have therefore imitated European education more than a rational policy would require. Schools and universities have channeled European types of knowledge to people who are to live under conditions very different from those of modern

Europe. Furthermore, some of the more well-to-do students go abroad and finish their education at universities and other institutions of higher learning in the rich countries. This has had two harmful effects. One is the well-known brain drain: a considerable number of highly educated people from LICs and MICs can utilize their acquired knowledge better either by going to HICs or staying there after graduating than by devoting themselves to tasks in their home countries. The other effect is perhaps even more harmful: in many poor countries a large effort is made to channel inappropriate kinds of knowledge to people, who cannot utilize it adequately.

A more appropriate educational system is therefore the best means of making sure that a selective policy of knowledge-transfer from technically more developed countries can be effective. Fortunately, there is a growing awareness of this in a number of LICs.

POLITICAL RELATIONS

Any intensification of the economic intercourse between countries makes them more dependent on one another. Governments must therefore increasingly consider how the situations of their countries are influenced by the economic policies of other countries, and how their own policies influence other countries. In this way the complications in economic relations among countries are rapidly increasing the number of political problems in each country's intercourse with the others.

This is a rather new development; in former times countries had rather little to do with one another except in wartime or in times of conflict or tensions that could lead to war. On the other hand such wars were rather frequent for a number of reasons, and some wars intensely influenced the further development of one or more countries.

A case in point is the series of wars that resulted from the great Arab expansion in the centuries after Mohammed. Even in our time we have seen important consequences of this expansion, such as the establishment of a number of Arab states in North Africa and West Asia, to some extent united in their relations with the rest of the world.

A more direct consequence of the post-Mohammed Arab expansion was that Europe was influenced by Arab culture. After the Crusades an intensification of Arab-European relationships led to a revival of European trade with India and other parts of Asia. New flows of armed expansion, this time Mongolian and Turkish, threatened these trade routes; this factor, combined with more knowledge about the world, encouraged Europeans to seek new ways to India. The ensuing Maritime Revolution led in its turn to an enormous expansion of European influence in the world, in the form of colonialism.

Barbara Ward has said that "the Westerners went to Asia not to conquer but to trade. Wherever local conditions were stable enough and local authority powerful enough to maintain order, no conquest occurred."[10] This is probably true; but when necessary the Europeans defended their trade by annexation of territory; and therefore their interference went particularly far where local political systems were weak or where various princes fought against one another. It is therefore nothing new that economic relations can create the background for important political change.

The most striking fact about colonialism, however, is the way in which it has been liquidated, with few exceptions and with remarkably little resistance on the part of the metropolitan countries. This is perhaps until now the most important result of the Egalitarian Revolution discussed in Chapter 3; at any event, the establishment of new independent states like India, Pakistan, Indonesia, and many others was one of the two spectacular results of the political situation after World War II.

The other great result of this situation was of course the Cold War, leading among other things to the domination by the USSR of Eastern European countries and to the introduction of socialist systems in these countries. The future of relations between socialist countries and other countries is one of the problems to be dealt with in Chapter 9, with due recognition of the difficulties involved.

It seems appropriate to conclude this chapter with some remarks about another important feature of world development after World War II. I am referring to the unique extension of regional and worldwide cooperation among states. This is yet another consequence of the knowledge expansion in the present phase of history. I have already commented on the way in which economic transactions are transcending national frontiers, thus leading to increasing interdependence of countries; at the same time, military techniques have developed in such a way that only the United States and the USSR have been able to set up systems that can be considered meaningful, if this word is still justified. Other countries can only provide reasonably meaningful security systems for themselves by pursuing policies that ensure some kind of support from one of the two superpowers.

Therefore we have the regional military or political groupings like NATO, the Warsaw Pact, and others. At the same time economic cooperation and coordination of policies have been furthered by the growing interdependence of countries. In this field too, regional groupings are playing an important role at the present stage.

We also have an elaborate system of worldwide organizations, centered around the United Nations. It is, however, difficult to bring about a far-reaching cooperation among more than one hundred countries, which are different in many respects. It is possible to proceed somewhat further in a restricted group of countries that have approximately the same economic structure and political system.

In some cases regional cooperation in such a restricted group has led to measures that could be carried through on a worldwide basis at a later stage. Liberalization of trade and payments was achieved in the Organization for European Economic Cooperation for countries of Western Europe in the years from 1948 to 1961. Later on such liberalization took place for a much wider group of countries under the auspices of GATT and the International Monetary Fund. Similarly, work on environmental problems was started in OECD, the successor of OEEC, extended to include the United States, Canada, Japan, and later on Australia and New Zealand. After a world conference in Stockholm in 1972 such work was taken up by the United Nations.

It seems then, that at the stage where we are a combination of regional and worldwide systems of international cooperation is appropriate. Often the results are far from satisfactory, but one should remember that this is a relatively new development. I think it is fair to say that the world situation is somewhat better and less disharmonious than it would be without such co-operation.

NOTES

1. *International Trade 1972* (Geneva, 1973).

2. *FAO Trade Yearbook 1971* (Rome: Food and Agricultural Organization).

3. World Bank, *Annual Report 1971*, Washington, D.C., p. 53.

4. Ibid.

5. World Bank, *Annual Report 1972*, Washington, D.C.

6. Development Assistance Committee, "Development Cooperation," *1973 Review* (Paris: OECD, 1973), p. 42.

7. United Nations, *Multinational Corporations in World Development* (New York: the UN, 1973), Table 42.

8. Ibid., p. 190.

9. Ibid., Table 42.

10. Barbara Ward, *Five Ideas that Changed the World* (London: Hamish Hamilton, 1959), p. 73.

8

THE DEVELOPMENT PROCESS

NATURE OF THE PROCESS

In Chapters 4 through 7 I have tried to combine theoretical considerations with a statistical analysis of recent development. This analysis has covered economic development, ten aspects of social development, population development, and international relations. The question now is how to put these pieces together and get a picture of the development process as a whole. In doing so I shall also try to give an answer to the question raised in the Introduction: Is there something that can be called the typical development process?

I think the answer is yes, though with some important modifications that will be dealt with in the next section. In this section I will concentrate on those features of the ongoing development that seem to be more or less general, insofar as they appear in all types of countries.

There are many such features; in fact the analysis has shown remarkable correlation among the various aspects of the development process considered, and the seven income groups of countries seem to represent stages of development in a number of respects. In a number of cases the changes observed when we move upward from the lower to the higher income groups correspond to those changes that take place in all or most of the groups when we move forward in time. We have also found considerable similarity in the ways in which several parts of the social system change in the process.

Roughly speaking, I think the typical development process can be characterized by the following twelve features:

1. Population grows.
2. With few exceptions production grows faster than population, so that income levels become higher.
3. Society becomes more and more differentiated. Agriculture employs a declining part of the labor force and services an increasing part. The percentage employed in industry increases up to a point and then decreases slowly.

4. Urbanization proceeds, so far apparently with no fixed ceiling.
5. On the whole, nutritional standards become higher, although on this point a modification is introduced below.
6. Housing standards also become higher, although with variations.
7. Energy consumption per capita increases.
8. Health service is gradually extended.
9. Life expectancy is extended, and infant mortality decreases substantially.
10. Education is extended at all levels, with secondary and higher education growing faster than primary education.
11. Politically, societies move towards the status of sovereign national states, so far with varying degrees of participation in decision making.
12. In international trade, exports of manufactures increase in proportion to exports of primary products in countries at all economic levels.

The last point mentioned means that most countries are becoming less dependent on the export situation of a single or a few primary products. This may be one of the reasons why the so-called developing countries now on the whole seem to be less dependent on the economic growth of the more industrialized countries than until recently was generally thought. It can be seen from Table 4.3 that in the years 1968-72 economic growth was slowing down in the industrialized countries but generally speeding up in the regions that have been described as developing.

In the same connection I have mentioned that a slowing down in the growth of development assistance from the rich countries did not appear to have any notable influence on the economic expansion of the receiving countries as a whole.

Too-firm conclusions should not be drawn from such changes in the apparent relationship of rich and poor countries over a short period, but if we look at the development process in its entirety as described above I think we will be justified in saying that medium income countries and low income countries are less dependent on what happens in high income countries than they used to be. They are also less dependent than it is assumed in some parts of the literature.

Development is something that goes on internally in a country. The export conditions for certain primary products are important for the balance of foreign payments at any point in time, but what matters more in the long run is the development of the country's agriculture, handicrafts, and other appropriate activities, including the building up of an infrastructure and of a generation so educated as to carry its progress further.

In this respect it should not be forgotten that by the early 1970s nearly all countries existing have been independent for at least a decade; most of them have had their independence for many years. There has therefore been time enough to build up political and administrative machinery, and experience has been gained by deliberate efforts to further economic and social development.

In these efforts the newly independent countries have been able to draw on the knowledge and insight accumulated by international organizations and in particular the specialized agencies of the UN system. They have also received technical assistance from industrialized donor countries. Although there has been a slowing down in the growth of development assistance, it should in fact be added that technical assistance has represented an increasing part of the flow of aid. There can be no doubt that the experience gained by the aid agencies, national and international, has enhanced the quality of the assistance.

In other words knowledge, the most important factor of development, has been available in growing amounts even in the poorer countries, where it has gradually increased the productivity of their human and material resources.

It must be added, however, that the typical development process is disharmonious in at least two important ways, and the disharmony created has often been a source of tension and conflict. Most important is probably the fact that inequality is increasing in the poorest countries, which represent the earlier phases of development. When an agricultural society begins to differentiate, inequality of income distribution begins to develop, as shown in the second section of Chapter 5. To this is added inequality of power, so that over long periods these societies are dominated by a class of big landowners, as seen in the tenth section of Chapter 5. When to this is added the emergence of a capital-owning bourgeoisie, we get the tension that is created by gaps in wealth and power, which can provoke revolution. It was at this point in European development that the socialist philosophy was originated.

In passing it is worth noting that at various earlier stages before the emergence of the bourgeoisie, peasants' revolts had already taken place in a number of European countries, but they were not strong enough to succeed.

This inequality of income and of power recedes in the later stages of the development process of those countries that have had a long and continuous evolution, participating in the "main stream of human progress" described in Chapter 3. However, inequalities are important features of most societies even today.

The other important source of disharmony in the typical development process has been excessive population growth. The demographic transition described in Chapter 6 means that death rates begin to go down when nutritional or other improvements make people more resistant to illness. This is then followed by falling birth rates at a later stage, but there may be a long period in which population growth is fairly rapid.

This growth brings about a pressure on resources. Historically this has led nomads to look for new pastures, and it has led to the periods of great migrations that have overthrown established empires, most often more civilized than the invaders.

In our own time excessive population growth is taking place in many of the poorer countries, while other countries are in various phases of the demographic transition, which takes on different forms in different types of societies. The same is true of other elements in the interaction of many factors that we call development. Since the countries in the world are at very different economic and technical levels, there are some rather different variants of the typical development process. This is the subject of the following section.

VARIANTS

Today there exist countries at very different economic levels, and they also differ in a number of other respects. Intercourse between these countries is being intensified by highly developed means of transport and communication, and as a consequence the development in each country is a mixture of what is homemade and what is due to influences from abroad. These influences work in various directions, but most of them spread from HICs to MICs and LICs.

It has been stressed at various places in this book that knowledge is the dynamic and most decisive factor of development. It has also been said that it is in the nature of knowledge to spread: in this respect it can be compared with water, which will flow from a basin with a higher level to one with a lower level if the two are connected. What was described in Chapter 3 as "transferred innovation" is exactly such a flow of knowledge.

There will usually be people on both sides who are interested in this flow. Enterprises in HICs may be interested in raw materials existing in a poorer country, or in cheap labor and new markets. In the poorer country both the government and many individuals have an interest in imitating things existing in the richer country and in learning how to obtain some of its advantages.

How these factors work, of course, varies from one country to another; each country is a special case. To get an impression of the spectrum of variants thus developing, I think it useful to compare two rather extreme cases, namely a typical HIC, with a long and continuous development achieved, and an LIC, in which the influence from HICs has not yet spread throughout society. The LIC is therefore a dual society in the sense indicated in the second section of Chapter 5.

In the typical HIC, the twelve special processes described in the previous section of this chapter will have been going on through many centuries. There has therefore in most cases been ample time for the adaptation required by, say, increasing urbanization or the establishment of new branches of industry or new systems of education. There may have been periods when the inequalities referred to above created tension or even provoked violent action, but that will usually have taken place in earlier phases of the process. Modern knowledge will on the whole be well adapted to the society as it is today, because this knowledge has developed gradually, along with a simultaneous development of society.

In a poor country with a dual society, much will be different. There will be a small modern sector applying techniques that have been transferred from HICs. Incomes in this sector will be much higher than those of the large traditional sector. There will also be a gap between the social status of people in the modern sector and that of other people. Usually there will also be a much higher average level of education in the modern sector than in the rest of the community, and there may be a cultural gap between those who have a Western type of education and those who have not. People employed in subsidiaries of a foreign corporation will have personal links with people abroad and perhaps relatively few similar links with people in the host country.

What makes it difficult for the fruits of modern knowledge to spread harmoniously in the LIC are a number of circumstances. First, this knowledge is on the whole ill-adapted to the situation of the country. The productive techniques of HICs have been developed in order to produce goods for which there is a demand in rich countries. Usually these techniques require much capital and a personnel having qualifications that are rare in the poor country.

The poor people in the countryside hear about this privileged modern sector. If they have gone to school they will often have received small bits of education of a Western type, and may therefore feel that they are qualified to be employed in the modern sector. We therefore get the well-known rural-urban migration, in which too many of the migrants become unemployed and are forced to live in houses built by themselves in miserable slums.

It should be added that the demographic transition starts in a more violent way in such countries than in the old societies of HICs, where it is a process stretching over a couple of centuries or more. In an LIC, health-service practices introduced from abroad may reduce mortality rapidly, and since birth rates will remain high for a rather long period, population growth can be very fast for quite a number of decades.

It was stressed in Chapters 4 and 5 that economic development is usually slow in LICs, and that inequality of income is increasing in the earlier stages of the development process. Added to the population growth this means that a rather large part of a rapidly growing population may remain very poor for a long time, the gap between these people and the privileged minority increasing rather than decreasing.

It is no wonder that there is unrest and political instability in such a society: situations often arise that provoke military intervention and there are therefore a number of military regimes in these dual societies.

Socialist countries, and I refer only to socialist societies in the narrower sense, such as those established through the Russian and the Chinese Revolutions, can be considered as representing a special variant of the development process. What is special about these countries is that they are introducing techniques taken over from abroad in a way that is totally controlled by government, and applying them in enterprises where, in principle, land and capital have been expropriated from the former owners. They therefore in the initial stages represent an extreme case of discontinuity. The inequalities stemming from the concentration of wealth in the possession of big landowners and capital owners from commerce and industry must in principle have been abolished in such societies; how much private ownership there remains can vary from case to case. Private plots in agriculture, private savings accounts, and a few other things do not change the system radically.

Hierarchical inequality is also bound to remain to some extent. China has tried to keep that at a minimum, but it may prove difficult to keep it there during the further development of Chinese society.

These are the main differences between socialist countries and other countries. In none of the many other aspects of development studied in Chapters 4 through 7 do the socialist countries stand out as radically different from nonsocialist countries at the same economic levels. To improve nutrition, housing, health, and education requires the same kinds of efforts whether a country is centrally planned or not. In any system, part of the results of production must be set aside for investment in capital, and in knowledge whether it be in the shape of research or in the educational system. The government of a socialist country has more power to decide how much to use for investment than the governments of other countries; some waste can also be avoided because advertising is unknown. On the other hand, society does not get the advantages of the many experimental initiatives that characterize private economic activities.

In recent years socialist countries have tried to get these advantages by some decentralization of power; leaders of state enterprises have then acted in ways more similar to those of managers in other countries.

At the same time nonsocialist countries have moved in the opposite direction, reducing inequality by such means as progressive taxation and social security systems, and public institutions in health service, education, and transportation. Private enterprise is subjected to public control in many ways.

In conclusion, it is important to stress that the description given above deals with extreme cases in order to underline the characteristic features of variants that are really different. This must not conceal the fact that in the actual world there are all kinds of intermediate cases. To a large extent the main features of the typical development process are found in all countries.

THE REGIONS

The patterns of development vary somewhat from one region to another. A look at the main regions of the world can therefore serve as a supplement to the previous section about variants of the typical development process. It can also throw some light on various economic and political relations between some of the regions that seem likely to be of importance in the future.

The following remarks refer to the main regions as they are defined in various tables in this book, such as Table 4.2. Details about the definitions are found in the Annex.

North America and Oceania

Geographically the four-country group made up of the United States, Canada, Australia, and New Zealand belongs to two regions and not to one. These countries are treated as one group here because they have some important characteristics in common. All of them are societies formed by European emigrants; the original inhabitants are now only small minorities. They have therefore inherited from Western Europe all the experience gained from the main stream of human progress. To what they have added the advantage of starting afresh in new surroundings. The territories they found are rich in natural resources: per capita this group of countries has more agricultural land than any of the other regions, and there are also considerable mineral resources.

As a result this "region" has a substantially higher level of GNP per capita than any other. Its consumption of raw materials per capita is therefore at a very high level, yet it is a net exporter of raw materials.

Of particular importance is the fact that this group of countries is by far the largest net exporter of food. As can be seen from Table 7.6, it is the only obvious food surplus area in the world; the relatively small surplus of Latin

America may be doubtful as a source of future supply because of the rapid population growth of that region. Furthermore, the nutritional standard of Latin America is not very high, and home consumption of food per capita should therefore increase considerably in the years to come. The USSR was a net exporter of cereals in 1969, but in a couple of later years it has had large net imports. As the world is today, one must therefore count on North America and Oceania for the supply of food to the deficit areas and in particular for additional supplies when there is an acute shortage in one region or another.

On the other hand this group of countries had a small net import of manufactures in 1969, in contrast to 1960 when there was a small surplus of exports. Part of the explanation probably is that the war in Vietnam and the Moon Race absorbed so much of the United States' productive and innovative capacity that industrial exports were weakened. In fact, a number of U.S. corporations made large investments abroad during the 1960s and transferred part of their production to Europe and Latin America instead of exporting from their home country. Since the devaluation of the U.S. dollar in the early 1970s the trade balance has improved, but the United States is bound to be affected by this tendency to move industrial production to countries with lower wage levels. This includes Canada, whose exports of manufactures increased substantially faster than those of the United States from 1960 to 1969.

In this respect it must be remembered that an increasing proportion of human and other resources in the United States is devoted to services, and the country is a big exporter of certain services, including technology sold in the forms of patents and license production.

Europe

"Europe," defined as the second region of HICs in this book, virtually means Western Europe. It is the largest net exporter of manufactures in the world, followed by Japan. At the same time it is by far the largest net importer of both food and raw materials, and in particular it is heavily dependent on imports of oil; its economy is therefore vulnerable. The consequences of higher oil prices will be discussed in Chapter 9. Here it is more pertinent to mention a couple of problems that have come up during the 1960s, at least in part because economic development was pushed by deliberately expansionist policies. I am referring to the growing rates of inflation and the growing concern about the environment. These problems are also felt in other industrial countries such as the United States and Japan, and of course to a more modest extent in many other countries as well.

They have a special character in Europe, however, because there they spread more easily from one country to another than anywhere else in the world. This is true of inflation because of the very large intro-European trade resulting from the two free trade arrangements in Western Europe, the EEC and EFTA. Environmental problems are also contagious in Europe because the countries are so close to one another: the Baltic Sea is polluted by rivers running through several countries, for instance, and the air in Scandinavia is polluted by the Ruhr industry in Western Germany. These are problems that may come up in other parts of the world in the course of further development.

Japan

What has just been said about Europe to a large extent applies to Japan as well. Japan has had a unique expansion of its industrial exports, but on the other hand it is even more dependent than Europe on imports of raw materials and fuel. It is also becoming an importer of food on a large scale because it has reached a level of incomes where the consumption of animal food begins to increase rapidly, something that can be noted now in various other MICs.

The USSR

USSR has a larger area than that of any other state, but it has less good agricultural land per capita than North America and Oceania, and it is exposed to very important climatic variations. It is therefore difficult to judge whether in the foreseeable future it will be a deficit or a surplus area regarding food.

For primary products as a whole it has been a net exporter, while it was a net importer of manufactures on a modest scale both in 1960 and 1969. A large part of its trade in both directions has been with other socialist countries, and this no doubt reflects a problem that is becoming acute both in the USSR and in some of the socialist countries in Eastern Europe.

In 1962 some 72 percent of the exports of countries belonging to the "Eastern Trading Area" went to other countries within that area. In 1972 this percentage had fallen to 62. At the same time the percentage of the imports coming from other countries within the group fell from 71 to 63.[1] There is thus a slowly growing trade with nonsocialist countries, but obviously the USSR and some Eastern European countries have now reached a stage in their development at which this is not enough. As stressed in Chapter 7 the more countries industrialize the more they trade with one another in industrial goods.

Since with the exception of Yugoslavia, the socialist countries have not until recently been members of the International Monetary Fund, they have been bound to settle most of their trade balances by internal trade, but there were limited possibilities, especially for a relatively highly industrialized country like Czechoslovakia, which therefore was interested in more trade with nonsocialist countries.

This was part of the background of the difficulties that led to the Soviet intervention in 1968, but now the USSR has itself entered into closer economic relations with both the United States and Japan, and its treaty with West Germany obviously has a similar purpose. It can be added that a few multinational corporations have been allowed to make investments in the USSR with

Soviet participation, and Romania has now joined the International Monetary Fund.

This liberalization of foreign economic relations must be seen as a step in the same direction as the decentralization of decision making mentioned in the last section of Chapter 5. It has not, however, brought with it a substantial increase in the freedom of expression of personal views in socialist countries. In this respect the system is still rather authoritarian, as are the systems of other one-party states or states with military regimes. We are obviously at a stage of development where it is unclear to what extent intensified international relations can influence the internal systems of countries with more or less authoritarian regimes.

Latin America

It has been stressed in various parts of this book that Latin American countries are still more in the nature of dual societies than one would expect in view of their average income level. Their exports of primary products suffered from the effects of the great depression of the 1930s, and some countries started a protectionist policy to further industrial production for import substitution; but investments by U.S. corporations took over a considerable part of the new industry that was started; and as mentioned in Chapter 5, industrial employment did not increase to the same extent that it did in other countries at the same economic level. In large parts of the region large-scale farming is still dominant, and the social structure is still marked by much inequality.

The relations with the United States have been much discussed. Apart from the U.S. investment, they have included a mixture of efforts on the part of various U.S. administrations to support Latin America, to win its friendship, and at the same time to have some influence on its political development. As an extension of the Monroe Doctrine, there has been a fear of socialist evolution in Latin America, which was supposed to contain a certain risk for the United States. The efforts of the United States to influence its southern neighbors culminated in the intervention in the Dominican Republic in 1965. There is something in this relationship on the American continents that reminds one of the relationship between the USSR and Eastern Europe. The efforts of the United States to influence its weaker neighbors have been much less far-reaching than Russia's in Eastern Europe, where the Brezhnev Doctrine has officially advocated a system of limited sovereignty for countries other than the USSR. The similarity lies in the intention of the United States to protect its own system by exerting influence in the countries from which it might be threatened.

The important thing about Latin America, in my view, is confirmed by the analysis undertaken in various chapters of this book, and that is that there has been too little internal development. If the Latin American countries in general had achieved a broader social development and strengthened the indigenous agriculture and exporting industry, they would have had stronger and more democratic political systems, and they would also have been more independent of foreign influence. Cuba has been able to maintain a socialist system since 1959, and a progressive military regime in Peru has in a remarkable way achieved a much broader social development than most other Latin American countries and has shown much independence in its foreign relations.

Other Medium Income Countries

The other MICs are spread all over the world, and therefore they are not a region. Two subgroups within this larger group of countries deserve a few comments.

Southern Europe

The countries of Southern Europe are now beginning to catch up with the HICs of Western Europe, but authoritarian regimes are preventing the economic advance from leading to a broader social development with freedom of expression.

The Oil Exporting Countries

The oil exporting countries are now earning very large amounts of foreign exchange, which they cannot use for speeding up the development process in their own societies without the collaboration of HICs and international organizations that can provide the knowledge required. The most difficult problem raised by the increases in oil prices is, however, their serious effect on the economies of some of the poorest countries of the world. The oil exporting countries are aware of this dilemma, but price discrimination in favor of some countries in not easily put into practice. Some new and difficult problems regarding international relations are therefore arising from the new price policy for oil. They will be discussed in Chapter 9.

Low Income Countries, Asia

This region is already the home of half of the world's population, and its population will continue to grow rather fast for a long time to come. There is already pressure on the land in a number of countries, and apart from exports of some tropical products the region is a net importer of food, so far on a modest scale. Natural resources are not particularly rich compared with the very large population, and capital formation in poor countries is bound to be modest.

What is abundant is labor, which can be utilized in a broad rural development, as is now tried in China, and in manufacturing for home consumption and for exports. Hong Kong, Taiwan, South Korea, and to some and for exports. Hong Kong, Taiwan, South Korea, and to some extent India and Pakistan have made some progress in this direction.

Educational standards are somewhat higher than in Africa, and societies are less dual than in Latin America. The conditions for attracting labor intensive industry from high-wage countries should therefore be fulfilled, provided confidence in political stability is sufficient. So far, however, a large part of the population still lives on small farms or as landless laborers in the villages. The future of this system is therefore to be looked at with great concern. This problem will be dealt with in Chapter 9.

Low Income Countries, Africa

Dual societies are widespread in Africa, and the population is still growing fast. There is also political instability in many parts of the continent, but there is more land per capita than in Asia, and therefore some of the problems are less acute.

There is an increasing interest in rural development in some African countries, and experimental attempts are being made to reduce urban-rural migration by intensifying agriculture and establishing small-scale industries in rural areas.

There is, however, no solution in sight for the special problem of white domination in Southern Africa, perhaps with the exception of the Portuguese territories. Pressure from other countries and from the United Nations on the governments in question has so far proved ineffective. The southern part of Africa is the most conspicuous illustration of a general dilemma that characterizes the present phase of world development. The ideas of the Egalitarian Revolution are now so widespread that it is considered a matter for international concern if fundamental human rights are violated by an authoritarian regime. There seems to be no means, short of military intervention, of forcing such a regime to change its policy, however. To make a boycott really effective seems to be nearly impossible. The sovereign national state is still the main decision-making unit, and a government that wants to defy world opinion can usually find some allies outside its own frontiers with whom to do business.

Much more could of course be said about the various regions. The purpose of this brief survey has only been to underline a few important features and point out policy problems that are closely related to the development process as such. It should therefore serve as a background for the discussion of the future that is the subject of Chapter 9.

NOTE

1. GATT, *International Trade 1972* (Geneva, 1973), Table 2.

9

THE FUTURE

Trends and Events

To what extent is the future predictable? If humanity has still millions of years to live on our planet, there is probably not much that can be said about the nature of human life during this long future. Even if we limit our considerations to what is sometimes called "the foreseeable future," a general theory of development can hardly even become a "theory of the future history." It cannot tell us, for instance, whether there will be a third world war. The question is, whether enough can be said about future possibilities to widen our understanding of the development process and make our thinking about future policies reasonably meaningful.

History can be considered as composed of trends and events. A number of trends can be noted at any time. Population grows at an annual rate that may be constant, rising, or falling. So do food production, maritime transport, and the number of telephone calls. Ideas about democracy or religion are changing, perhaps in wave-like ups and downs, perhaps in the same direction throughout a rather long period, or perhaps in some other way.

However, events of a more or less unique nature happen, and they may influence trends in a way that seems unpredictable, the events themselves being even more unforeseeable. One could hardly have foreseen the coming on the scene of Napoleon or Hitler, or the murder in Sarajevo in 1914 that started the first world war.

Such events of course limit our possibilities of making reliable statements about the future. The question is to what extent this is the case. Without going into a discussion about "historicism," it may be appropriate to make three observations about the relations between trends and events.

1. Trends are in fact composed of events, each of them being small compared with the whole stream. The individual events may be unpredictable, but because of their large number a certain statistical regularity may neverthe-

less be noted. It cannot be foreseen whether a certain person will die in a certain year or whether a certain family will have a child, but the total number of deaths and births seldom changes in a very abrupt way. A person may change his mind about democracy somewhat when reading an article in a newspaper, but it is unlikely that the majority of a large population will change its mind very much overnight.

There is no sharp distinction between such events, which are so small that they are entirely obscured by the trends and by events that disturb the regularity of development somewhat more. Changing weather conditions can mean fluctuations in harvests, but seldom affect them enough to influence the trends in food production. However, two consecutive bad harvests in India in 1965 and 1966 because of disappointing monsoons made a noticeable slow-down in the economic growth of that large country. On the other hand they have pushed the efforts to improve farming methods so much that their long-term effects are doubtful and may be positive. These improvements would probably have come anyway, but perhaps later if the monsoon had been normal in the two years mentioned. This case, then, seems to be on the borderline between the small happenings that can be considered elements of a trend and the more unique "events" that apparently sometimes change the course of history.

2. Concerning these latter events two considerations are in order. The first is that even if the event itself is not foreseeable it will often have been preceded by trends that lead to "tensions," wherein the disharmonies take on such dimensions that people with foresight begin to expect that something dramatic may happen.

The murder in Sarajevo was not foreseen by anyone other than those who planned it, but in the years up to 1914 there were growing tensions among the major powers in Europe. Knowledgeable students of society were therefore not unaware that a war could break out if the dominant trends were not changed.

People with mental structures like those of Napoleon and Hitler, are probably born now and then in various countries, but one never hears about them because the tensions do not arise that can bring them into power. Such tensions did, however, exist in France after ten years of revolution and war; and they existed in Germany after the defeat in 1918, the difficulties in creating a viable democracy, and then the bad effects of the Great Depression.

Similarly, although the concrete events that led to the independence of Bangladesh could hardly have been foreseen, tensions between East and West Pakistan had developed in such a way that students of history were not surprised when radical changes took place.

A careful study of major trends, therefore, can often sharpen the aware-ness of rising tensions in such a way that seemingly unforeseeable "unique" events become less surprising. What is more, if such an awareness leads to wise policies these events may not happen at all.

3. The other important fact regarding "unique" events is that they probably on the whole influence the long-term trends of history much less than would appear at first sight. This certainly was the case as far as Napoleon's activi-ties are concerned and most likely also concerning Hitler's, though in this case we have not yet seen the full long-term effects.

If an apparently unique event has really important long-term effects, it seems more likely than not that the event was only a concrete occasion that brought about something that was rooted in forces that had been at work for years. The murder in Sarajevo is a case in point.

A study of trends should therefore be rewarding. A simple extrapolation of recent trends is seldom enough, except for very short periods. Trends are the result of complicated interactions among many factors, and only a careful study of these factors and the nature of the relationships among them can make it possible to form an opinion about the trends in question that reaches some time into the future. In some cases quantitative projections can then be useful, perhaps in the form of maximum and minimum values for certain magnitudes. Often, however, qualitative evaluations are more appropriate. Is it likely or not, for instance, that there will be a convergence between the politicoeconomic systems of Eastern and Western Europe?

How far should we try to look into the future? In order to answer this question it is useful to remember that we seem to approach a period during which some major trends will begin to change in an important way. We have gone through a couple of centuries of unusual expansion in knowledge, population, and the production of goods and services, and in the last few decades this expansion has further accelerated. Given the limited size of our planet it is obvious that this cannot go on forever. If we are to think of the future of man's history in terms of millions of years, no higher average rate of population growth than zero will be possible. Roughly speaking the same must apply to production of goods, which increasingly must be based on a recycling of materials and on sources of energy that are not exhausted.

A gradual slowing down of some of the present trends can therefore be foreseen. Some trends will change sooner and faster than others, and one of the questions it will be particularly important to study is how we can manage to accomplish this transition to a period of less rapid growth and what its timing will be. Based on our present knowledge it would seem reasonable to expect that the 21st century will see an important change in that direction.

This being so, it seems appropriate to distinguish between two periods as a matter of principle, although they will overlap to a large extent in the practical course of events.

The next section of this chapter deals with medium-term trends, or the possible trends in a period in which presumably the forces now at work will not have changed radically. The section following it, on the other hand, discusses some of the problems that are likely to come up in a later period, in which under favorable circumstances the transition to a reasonably stable world-society could gather momentum. This would imply a movement towards a stationary world population and a slowing down of the expansion of material production to such an extent that exhaustion of resources and deterioration of the environment would cease.

As already indicated, the distinction between two periods is more a convenient way of separating different types of trends than a question of timing properly speaking, because in actual fact the two "periods" will overlap to a large extent. If, nevertheless, a rough indication were to be given, one could probably venture to say that the remainder of the 20th century seems likely to be dominated by what are here called medium-term trends. In the 21st century the longer-term problems should on the whole be dominating.

In the years to come, the medium-term trends will raise a number of complicated policy porblems. Will it be a further complication to have the longer-term problems in view when present policies are formulated? The answer is probably, yes and no. There can be no doubt, however, that policies in the first period will be more meaningful if they are seen as preparation for a future that is a little further away. This at least is the fundamental idea on which the discussion of policy issues in the last section of this chapter is based.

MEDIUM-TERM TRENDS

It happens that this is written at a time when some important trends are particularly difficult to evaluate, even for a limited period. The recent, quite extraordinary rise in oil prices will influence both energy consumption and international relations in a way that has no precedent, for instance, and the importance of the recent reductions in birth rates in a number of HICs is also hard to judge, since they may be the beginning of a new long-term trend, or a certain reaction may reverse them later on.

Energy

The so-called oil crisis of 1973 is an "event" in the sense discussed in the previous section: The short war between Israel and a few Arab states occasioned a sharp rise in oil prices that may be permanent; the result has been the introduction of an unusual element of discontinuity in the development of the oil market.

Like most other major events this was not entirely unforeseeable, nor was it completely unforeseen. The events of 1973 had been preceded by a number of smaller events that, taken together, represent a trend. In 1960 five oil-producing countries formed the Organization of Petroleum Exporting Countries (OPEC). During the following 11 years six other countries joined, and in 1971 OPEC managed to get substantially higher prices from the oil companies, plus an agreement on further increases in the following years. Also, some oil-producing countries took over an increasing part of the equity capital of the oil companies operating in their territory.

This new policy became possible because the development of alternative sources oi energy had been disappointing for a number of years. Oil can be extracted from tar sands or from oil shales, and also from the bottom of the sea in various places, but in all these cases costs will be very much higher than in the Persian Gulf reservoirs out of which the main part of the oil now comes. Therefore the oil producers in that area have maintained a quasi-monopolistic position. At the same time the development of nuclear energy production proved to be much slower than was expected some years ago. There has been a growing concern about the risks of nuclear fission, which also requires very large investments. No rapid evolution can therefore be expected in this field.

Other possibilities are nuclear fusion and direct utilization of solar energy, which may become the major sources of energy in the long run. This may perhaps apply in particular to solar energy, which is our only real source of "income" in the energy field and therefore of a more permanent nature. For the moment we are living on our "capital," extracting fossil fuels from the soil.

There is, however, a long way to go before nuclear fusion and solar energy can be developed on a large scale. As a consequence the total supply of energy may become much smaller during the next few decades than the rapid increase during the 1960s would seem to indicate. In a 1973 expert report on the subject it was said that

> The rapid energy growth rates that most industrial countries have long maintained cannot continue for much longer. . . . Even the ability to maintain current levels of per capita energy conversion in many rich countries over the next few decades is in doubt.[1]

If a sharp reduction in the trend in this important field were to take place, two questions would arise. The first is how the reduction would be distributed in countries at various levels of income. To the extent that the poorest countries were hit, the consequences could be rather serious for their economic development. In the richer countries much of the energy is used for home comforts, such as heating, light, and air conditioning. The second question therefore is to what extent the reduction in the consumption of energy can be concentrated in these fields. If this is possible and acceptable to a high degree, production in agriculture and industry will be affected less; but it is impossible to say how the actual development will prove to be. It is unavoidable that a sharp reduction in the growth rates for energy consumption will entail some reduction in the rates of economic growth, but it is uncertain how this will work in the various income groups of countries.

In this respect it is important to note that the new increases in the price of oil will have a spectacular influence on the world's capital markets. Until recently the HICs plus Japan have had an annual balance-of-current-payments surplus on the order of 10 billion dollars; this has been used to finance their aid programs and private capital exports to the "developing countries," which had a deficit of the same order of magnitude. This will now change radically.

It has been estimated that because of the price increases, the main oil exporting countries will gain some 50 to 60 billion dollars per year extra. The corresponding losses for the oil importers have been estimated at something in the order of 35 billion dollars for the HICs and Japan, and 15 billion for the developing countries. These evaluations are of course very uncertain. It seems unavoidable, however, that most oil importing countries will now have large balance-of-payments deficits for a number of years to come.

These deficits will be financed through various channels by the oil exporting countries themselves, who may increase their own imports of various goods somewhat. They are bound to have a large surplus, however, which will flow into various parts of the international capital market.

This at least is what will happen in the early phases of the new development. What will happen later on is more uncertain; the oil exporting countries may make investments in the industry of high income countries, and they may start aid programs in poor countries. Gradually their own imports may increase, and according to some estimates their oil exports may reach their highest level in the early 1980s. Even if that should happen they will accumulate very large investments abroad, and later on they will earn substantial incomes from these investments.

The question is how the economies of other countries will be influenced by the corresponding deterioration of their foreign exchange positions. All the main oil exporters except Nigeria are medium income countries. All the main importers are high income countries, but a number of low income countries are dependent on oil imports, and the new situation is already a matter for concern in India.

It is hardly conceivable that most HICs can go on running a large balance-of-payments deficit for many years, and they are therefore likely to try slowly to correct the imbalance. Combined with the limited and more expensive supply of energy, this will have a negative influence on their rates of economic growth. It is to be feared that something similar will happen in oil importing LICs, but it is impossible to make a real quantitative evaluation of these new trends at the present moment.

The Birth Rate

The same is true of the new trend in population development. Perhaps one should not speak of a new trend at all, but rather of a sharp reinforcement of trends that have been at work for a long time. Birth rates have been going down slowly for nearly 200 years in HICs as a group, but recently this decrease has gathered momentum. For all HICs combined, the natural increase of population was only 65 percent in 1970, compared with 1.02 percent in 1960. For the European countries alone, the rate for 1970 was only .45 percent.

The main factors behind this rapid decline are an extensive use of new contraceptives and of induced abortion. The question is whether this trend will continue or whether a certain reaction will set in and provoke a retardation in the movement towards zero population growth. In Denmark the present fertility rates will lead to a slight decrease in total population in some years time if they continue.

In Romania changing attitudes towards abortion have strongly influenced procreation: liberal legislation during the 1950s was followed by restrictive measures in 1966, and as a result the birth rate per 1,000 inhabitants developed as follows:

	Birth Rate
1957	23
1966	14
1967	27
1971	19

These violent fluctuations make it hard to discern a clearly defined long-term trend.

That overall trends in HICs are pointing downward can hardly be questioned, and the movement in that direction might well be reinforced by the slowing down of economic growth resulting from the new situation concerning energy. However, projections for the next few decades cannot at this moment be much more than guesswork.

Two Assumptions About Medium-Term Trends

We are therefore faced with particularly great difficulties if at this juncture we try to evaluate medium-term trends concerning two of the more important aspects of the development process; economic development and population development.

This being so, I have found that the best thing to do was to make two rather different "assumptions" concerning the growth of population and of GNP, from the base year of this study, 1967, to the year 2000. These assumptions represent a pessimistic and an optimistic evaluation of the general trend from the point of view that is basic to the present study: Are we moving towards increasing disharmony or towards increasing harmony in the world community? Admittedly these two assumptions are arbitrary; I have deliberately chosen them in such a way that the differences between them are considerable. This should help to make the implications of moving in one direction or another clear.

The question is, what should be considered pessimistic and optimistic assumptions, respectively? I have found that the following considerations might be relevant in this respect.

Concerning population, the present decade seems to be the one in which the growth rate for world population will be the highest. From a UN report prepared for the World Population Conference in 1974[2] the following rates can be calculated (in percent per year):

	Growth Rate
1950-70	1.9
1970-85	2.1
1985-2000	1.8

For the period 1967-2000 I have chosen 2 percent as the more pessimistic Assumption 1, and 1.8 percent as the more optimistic Assumption 2. It is obvious that a slowing down of population growth is necessary in the long run, as well as highly desirable for the next few decades.

It is more difficult to decide what to assume for economic development. As mentioned above, it seems likely that the energy supply will grow much more slowly during the next few decades than it did during the 1960s. There may also be a shortage of some raw materials, and concern about the environment is likely to put a brake on the expansion of production in some fields. In any case, economic growth during the 1960s was exceptionally fast, and it is wise to be prepared for a substantial slowing down.

I have put the growth rate of GNP for the period 1967-2000 at 4.5 percent per year under Assumption 1 and 4 percent per year under

Assumption 2, compared with 5.3 percent for the 1960s for the 118 countries covered by Table 4.2.

Further details about these assumptions are found in the Annex. Here it may be appropriate to state why I have chosen the lowest growth rate for the most optimistic of the two assumptions; there are two reasons why I think this is reasonable. The first is that in the long run we must probably prepare for something close to a zero growth rate, not only for world population but also for other phenomena, such as the use of raw materials, the conversion of energy, the number of motor cars, and the quantity of polluting activities. Otherwise there can be no acceptable world for our descendants to live in in the centuries and millennia to come. The transition to such a stable future society will be easier if we have a gradual slowing down of economic expansion from now on, instead of putting the brakes on abruptly at a later date.

The other reason I chose the lowest growth rate as the most optimistic is that the most important development problem for the next century probably is how to give the LICs a fair chance to catch up with the richer countries, which now occupy the bulk of the world's resources of food, energy, and raw materials. A considerable slowing down of their rapid expansion should therefore make it easier for the really poor nations to get at least a somewhat more decent share of the resources of the earth than at present. As a consequence, Assumption 2 contains a more favorable growth rate for the LICs than Assumption 1, though the overall growth rate is lower.

Table 9.1 describes the development of population and of GNP during the period 1967-2000, as well as the situation in the year 2000, as they would be according to these two assumptions. The GNP figures are calculated in 1967 prices, and the table can therefore be compared with Table 4.2, which also describes the three main categories of countries. The table covers the same 118 countries that are covered by Table 4.2.

There are two aspects of the future development that this table throws some light on. The first is the utilization of the world's natural resources, which under both assumptions will be much more intensive in the year 2000 than it was in 1967, when the total GNP was $2,075 billion. Even if the overall growth rate of Assumption 2 were reduced from 4 to 3 percent, the total GNP would be as high as $5,500 billion in the year 2000.

There can therefore be no doubt that the consumption of energy, raw materials, and food will be at much higher levels at the end of the century if economic growth is to continue in a way that has even a slight resemblance to the one we have been accustomed to in recent years. In the richer countries the consumption of raw materials is growing more slowly than GNP, but energy consumption has on the whole grown at least as much as GNP.

An indirect consequence of such an increase in production will be that man's impact on the environment may reach dangerous levels. One of the trends of the near future will of course be an increase in the efforts to reduct the polluting effects of certain activities, but there are limits to the possibilities in this field if the volume of these activities is to grow to something close to even the lowest of the two assumptions.

During the last few years it has been increasingly felt in the richest countries that rapid economic growth and high levels of production are not

TABLE 9.1

Growth of Population and GNP, 1967-2000

	Annual Growth 1967-2000 (percent)			Population in the Year 2000 (millions)	GNP in the Year 2000 (billions of 1967 dollars)	GNP per Capita in the Year 2000 (1967 dollars)
	Population	GNP	GNP per Capita			
Assumption 1						
HICs	0.6	3.4	2.8	660	3,800	5,760
MICs	1.7	6.2	4.4	1,580	4,240	2,680
LICs	2.4	4.5	2.1	4,260	800	190
Average	2.0	4.5	2.5	6,500	8,840	1,360
Assumption 2						
HICs	0.3	2.5	2.2	600	2,940	4,900
MICs	1.5	5.8	4.2	1,480	3,740	2,530
LICs	2.2	5.0	2.7	4,000	940	240
Average	1.8	4.0	2.2	6,080	7,630	1,250

Source: Compiled by the author.

unmixed blessings. If during the next generation we are to raise GNP per capita to twice its present level or more, there is bound to be growing concern about a number of environmental problems.

There may be even more concern about the other aspect of the future development that is illustrated by Table 9.1. Under both assumptions the LICs will remain very poor at the end of the century; under both assumptions they will also represent about two-thirds of the world's population. To this is added the psychologically and politically important fact that the gap between these countries and the MICs will widen substantially.

Of course, other assumptions could be chosen. It is tempting to be optimistic in statements about the poor countries, but I feel that international organizations have sometimes yielded too much to this temptation. Further-more, the picture has been blurred in the past because no distinction has been made between MICs and LICs. The commonly used expression "developing countries" has contributed much to this confusion.

Of course, some of the present LICs are better placed than others in the future race for higher standards of living. This is true of those that are relatively well endowed with natural resources. The largest of these countries are already densely populated, however, and will be more so in the future. This applies to China, if we take into account that much of its territory is mountainous, and to such countries as India, Pakistan, and Bangladesh.

Nothing in the study undertaken in this book indicates that it would be realistic to make assumptions under which LICs as a group could catch up in a significant way with the richer countries during the remainder of the 20th century. They might be able to catch up with the richest countries if, for the reasons mentioned above, economic growth in, say, North America and Western Europe were slowing down as much as shown under Assumption 2 or more. But the indications are that the LICs would in any case lose ground compared with most MICs.

It must of course be added that this comparison with the more wealthy nations is only part of the picture. Under both of the assumptions made, LICs will on the average be considerably better off in the year 2000 than they were in 1967. They will nevertheless remain very poor societies, and it should not be forgotten that income distribution is very unequal in many of these countries. It may even become more unequal for some time to come, for the reasons discussed in the second section of Chapter 5. The poorer part of the population in large parts of Asia and Africa may therefore remain extremely poor for a long time. This applies to those that will be unemployed much of the time. It also applies to the small farmers, and this may be the place for a discussion of the increasing pressure on the land in some of these countries.

In Table 5.8 it is shown that number of hectares of agricultural land per capita of the agricultural population was as follows in the countries covered:

HICs	13.0
MICs	2.5
LICs	0.6

For North America and Oceania the figure is 42.2 hectares; while for the USSR it is 43.3 hectares; but for LICs in Asia it is only .4 hectares. These disparities will increase for many years to come. In HICs the agricultural population is going down, but in most LICs it is likely to increase substantially during the next couple of decades. The agricultural population of Asia and Africa was 781 million in 1950; by 1970 it had grown to 1,053 million.[3] It is therefore to be expected that there is still a long way to go before it will begin to decrease.

Not only are millions of farms in the poorest countries very small, but in many countries they are also split up into a number of even smaller plots, spread over the areas belonging to their villages. This of course makes farming highly inefficient. It must be added that in some countries land reform aims at creating more small farms by expropriation of land from the bigger estates. Although this may appear desirable from a social point of view, it sometimes has a negative effect on efficiency.

The pressure on the land in densely populated LICs is therefore closely related to the crucial question of the nutritional standard in two respects. The nutritional standard is low because there are so many poor people, but it is also low because food production is too small.

This leads us to the fundamental problem of the prospects for food demand and supply. In the long run this may be the most important of all development problems, but in this section I shall confine the considerations made, to medium-term trends as they might appear.

In the Annex it is explained how the quantities of food consumed can be expressed in terms of primary calories; that is, the calories represented by the food and feed crops needed for the production of the vegetable and animal food consumed by people.

In Table 9.2 the number of primary calories consumed in 1967 according to Table 5.11 is compared with the number required in the year 2000 according to Assumptions 1 and 2. The table describes the total demand for food as it would be according to the two assumptions. In order to meet this demand the production of food and feed crops would have to be as follows in the year 2000, if the figure for 1967 = 100:

Assumption 1	268
Assumption 2	257

A very substantial increase in food production would thus be required. What are the possibilities for getting so much more out of the agricultural land and the other sources available? At present fish and other seafood represents some 2 percent of the calories consumed, but around 15 percent of the animal protein. There is already a risk of overfishing in some waters, and it may be difficult for the supply of seafood to keep pace with the demand for food. Production of food on the land will therefore probably have to increase at least as fast as indicated above, under the two assumptions on which these considerations are based.

The area of agricultural land is going down slowly in many HICs because of such factors as urbanization and extension of roads. In MICs and LICs it is still increasing because new land is being taken up for cultivation. FAO has

TABLE 9.2

Food Consumption, 1967 and 2000

	Per Capita		Total Primary calories		
	Calories	Animal Protein (grams)	Animal (billions)	Vegetable (billions)	Total (billion)
1967	2,390	21.1	10,100	4,800	14,900
HICs	3,100	58.0	4,400	1,000	5,400
MICs	2,710	27.5	3,500	2,000	5,500
LICs	2,040	7.9	2,200	1,800	4,000
2000, Assumption 1	2,520	31.4	28,700	12,300	41,000
HICs	3,200	70	6,500	1,200	7,700
MICs	3,100	65	14,400	2,800	17,200
LICs	2,200	13	7,800	8,300	16,100
2000, Assumption 2	2,540	31.4	26,700	11,600	38,300
HICs	3,100	70	5,900	1,000	6,900
MICs	3,100	60	12,400	2,800	15,200
LICs	2,250	15	8,400	7,800	16,200

Source: Compiled by the author.

made some proposals regarding the increases that should take place during the period 1962-85.[4] The annual increases proposed for the decade 1975-85 are somewhat lower than those proposed for the years 1962-75. Based on these trends I have calculated tentative figures for the year 2000, as seen in Table 9.3, where they are compared with the corresponding figures for 1967. (See Table 5.8.) The figures for the year 2000 are based on the "optimistic" Assumption 2, concerning population.

This, then, is the land on which food will have to be produced under the assumptions stated. If we compare these figures with the figures concerning food consumption contained in Table 9.2, Assumption 2, we get the number of primary calories consumed per hectare of agricultural land in 1967 and 2000. This is shown in Table 9.4.

It can be seen from this table that for the world as a whole the production of food and feed per hectare would have to be more than twice its 1967 size in the year 2000 under the assumptions stated (Under Assumption 1 the index would be 243 instead of 227.) This would require sharply increased inputs of fertilizers and pesticides, and the ecological consequences would deserve very serious consideration.

The table also shows that if the three categories of countries were to be self-sufficient in food to the same degree in the year 2000 as they were in

TABLE 9.3

Agricultural Land, 1967 and 2000

	Total Area (millions of hectares)		Area per capita (hectares)	
	1967	2000	1967	2000
HICs	536	520	.99	.87
MICs	850	980	.94	.66
LICs	777	950	.44	.24
Total	2,163	2,450	.64	.40

Source: Compiled by the author.

TABLE 9.4

Consumption of Primary Calories per Hectare of Agricultural Land, 1967 and 2000*

	1967	2000	In 2000 (1967=100)
HICs	1,008	1,327	132
MICs	647	1,612	249
LICs	515	1,705	331
Average	689	1,563	227

*A small part of the land is used for beverages and tobacco but it is not changing much. The percentage of agricultural output consisting of food and feed would be:

	1960	1980
High income countries	92.5	94.1
Developing countries	86.5	87.8

Source: FAO Agricultural Commodity Projections 1970-80, Vol. I, Table 7.

1967, a modest increase in output would suffice in the HICs, while the increase would have to be very large in the MICs and even larger in the LICs. However, the three categories were not all self-sufficient to the same degree in 1967. It was shown in Chapter 7 that North America, Australia, and New Zealand were the absolutely dominating net exporters of food. (See Table 7.6.) This would seem to be increasingly the case during the remainder of this century, since there is no other major food reservoir in the world.

Latin America was a net exporter of food, to a small extent in cereals and in a more important way in meat, in 1967, but since rapid increase of population will continue in this region for a long time to come, the area as a whole can hardly be expected to have a food surplus of any importance at the end of the century. It seems reasonable to assume that both Latin America and the USSR will roughly speaking be self-sufficient in food at that time.

The main net importers of food in 1967 were Europe, Japan, and the LICs in Asia. This is likely to remain the case at the end of the century. Because of very slow population growth, Europe should need only a modest increase in her imports. The largest net importer of food in the year 2000 should therefore be the LICs in Asia, if nothing happens that can influence present trends in a spectacular way.

The trends will of course be influenced by future technological development in food production. Much has been done to improve techniques in agriculture during the years after World War II, but the results are difficult to measure. A reasonably good indicator is perhaps the yield of all cereals (100 kilograms per hectare), which was as follows:[5]

	1948-52	1971	1971 (1948-52=100)
HICs	16.7	31.1	186
MICs	9.6	16.1	168
LICs	9.8	14.5	148
Average	11.3	18.1	160

Relatively, the HICs have made the most rapid advance. In all three categories the progress was of course in part due to an increased use of fertilizers. The application of nitrogenous fertilizers, measured in kilograms of nitrogen per hectare, can serve as an example.[6]

	1948-52	1970/71
HICs	5.0	27.1
MICs	1.3	12.4
LICs	0.3	8.1
Average	2.0	14.5

This increase in the use of fertilizers has been favored by a decline in the price of energy compared with prices in general, since energy is a fairly important input in the production of fertilizers. The drastic increase in energy prices that has taken place in 1973-74 may therefore hamper further progress in this direction. The same is true of the sharp increase in the price of phosphate rock, also an important input in the production of fertilizers.

Unfortunately this is likely to have its strongest impact in the LICs, where the use of fertilizers is still at a low level. In a number of HICs the application of fertilizers is now at such high levels that further increases will have only a very modest effect. There is of course room for much improvement of agricultural techniques in most LICs, but adaptation of temperate zone technology is needed, and though increased use of irrigation and of multiple cropping can be expected, the supply of water may be a limiting factor in important parts of the tropical and subtropical zones.

Two concluding remarks about agricultural food production are therefore appropriate. The first is that it will probably not be an easy task to increase the world's total agricultural production to the extent needed to meet the demand in the year 2000 without important ecological side-effects. The other is that it is hard to see how the larger part of the Asian LICs can increase their food production to an extent that corresponds to the increase in their food consumption, until the end of the century. It would therefore, on the basis of present knowledge, seem to be most likely that they will become net importers of food to an increasing extent.

It remains to make a few remarks about nonagricultural food production. Experiments are being made in various technological fields, but most of them are probably more relevant in relation to the long-term problems to be discussed in the following section, than they are with regard to medium-term prospects. There seems to be one exception, however, namely the feeding of single cell organisms on petroleum or on other organic substrates. This is becoming a source of protein of some importance for the feeding of domestic animals, and existing information seems to indicate that it may be used as an element in various combinations of food for direct human consumption in the fairly near future. In the early stages such technological innovation will probably be most important in HICs. It may, however, become a new source of income for oil-producing countries, since it can be linked to the refining of petroleum.

Other Medium-Term Trends

The trends discussed so far are those that are most directly related to the average standards of living and to the most elementary necessities of life. There are of course many other trends that can be discerned by a careful analysis of the development process. It is therefore appropriate to take a look at the possible medium-term prospects in a few of the more important of these other fields.

The expansion of knowledge is likely to continue, but it may well be more difficult than in the recent past to get rapidly increasing funds for research in HICs, which will have deficits in their foreign payments because of the increased oil prices. This being so, science policies are likely to become more selective. Much effort will be devoted to the development of new sources of energy, as well as to energy-saving methods of production. Environmental problems will also be the subject of much research in HICs, and the same is true of economic and social questions such as inflation, the role of multinational corporations, and the use of narcotics.

Many HICs are passing through a difficult phase of their development. They are therefore likely to allocate the overwhelming part of their intellectual resources to their own internal problems. It may be a symptom of this "development disease" of the rich countries, that after a decade of unique economic expansion they were unwilling to agree to the fixation of a target for their own contribution to the research regarding problems of developing countries, when the strategy for the Second United Nations Development Decade was being defined.

If we look for a clue to the question of why the richest countries of the world can have a development disease, I think the answer is that knowledge, the dominant factor of development, is expanding in a disharmonious way.

Modern technological knowledge has made so many things technically feasible that even the resources of rich countries can only make it possible for us to have a small part of them. Modern advertising and political propaganda, also products of the knowledge expansion, are increasing the craving for goods and services, and therefore all kinds of pressure groups are asking for larger shares of the national product. At the same time, new techniques are forcing producers to make expensive investments, since their competitors are likely to do the same; and military technology is forcing the Western and the Eastern bloc to compete in the development of ever more sophisticated weapons.

The interaction of all these factors explains why the governments of the rich countries have been unable to cope with the problems of an accelerating inflation, and why they were unprepared for the shock they got when the oil exporting countries discovered how strong their temporary monopoly power is. More generally, one can say that politicians are so preoccupied by the questions of today that they are unable to give sufficient thought to the problems of tomorrow and the day after. It is easy to blame the politicians, but it is only fair to recognize that their difficulties reflect a fundamental disharmony in he development of knowledge.

Why are we becoming the slaves of technological progress instead of being its masters? I think the answer is that we lack what might be called knowledge about the way in which knowledge should be produced and utilized.

It cannot be repeated too often that knowledge is something that is being produced. Within wide margins we can decide in which directions this production is to develop. Subjected to human motivation it has developed in many different directions, guided by the desire for higher incomes, for prestige, for military strength, or for security. But there has not been time to gain a sufficient breadth of view, and this is dangerous in a phase of history in which the individual countries, and the individual groups within each country, are becoming increasingly interdependent.

Fortunately, there is a growing awareness of this lack of harmony, but it is unlikely that this will influence policies in a noticeable way during the next decade or more. The new balance of payments difficulties of western industrial countries, resulting from the oil crisis, are bound to make them more inward-looking, and these difficulties will create some conflicts of interest between countries that will weaken their ability to take joint action in world affairs.

It follows that the poorest countries can hardly count on a very active outside support, in a period in which they too will have extreme balance of payments difficulties because of the oil crisis. What under these circumstances will be their own internal development?

Their educational systems should continue to expand, and the same is true of their usually very modest capacity for doing research. Multinational corporations are also likely to make more investments in these countries, transferring technical knowledge to them and training a small but growing part of their labor force.

More important, perhaps, is the slowly growing awareness of the unhappy consequences of recent disharmonious development. Programs are being started to further rural development, and the suspicion that labor intensive techniques are invented to keep the poor countries down is receding in various countries. There is also a certain interest in making education better adapted to the real situation of the countries concerned. Vocational training and cautious experiments with functional literacy for adults are important elements of the new development in the field of education.

The main question about the next couple of decades is whether a real breakthrough can be expected for these efforts to get a more harmonious development, through a courageous drive towards adaptive innovation on a large scale.

The new balance of payments difficulties created by the increase in oil prices could serve as an appropriate motivation for such a drive. There are strong arguments for saving foreign exchange by avoiding the importation of expensive machinery where possibilities exist to use simpler equipment that can be produced at home and that would give employment to more people who would otherwise be unemployed. Likewise, materials existing in a country could in a number of cases replace imported materials, if appropriate techniques were developed.

Work is being done along these lines by institutions in a number of LICs, supported by aid agencies in some HICs and by international organizations. There are, however, many obstacles to overcome. The techniques that would be appropriate are to a large extent nonexistant today. Too many people have had inappropriate training, and too few are able to give the right kind of advice.

Our knowledge is still fundamentally imperfect about the essential question how to accomplish the transition to a more continuous and harmonious process of development that would include the entire society. What was said above about knowledge in general also applies to the specific branches of knowledge needed to prepare such a harmonious development. There is a lack of knowledge of a higher order, such as knowledge about the direction to give to the production and utilization of knowledge.

Results are therefore likely to vary considerably from one country to another. In dual societies the modern sector should gradually broaden somewhat, while agriculture and some related industries should make progress in the rural areas. Unemployment is likely to increase in many countries for a rather long time to come, however, and the fragmentation of agricultural holdings will create a class of small farmers who are unable to take much advantage of new technical developments. It has sometimes been argued that animal husbandry would be a field in which small farmers would have a comparative advantage, but some recent research seems to indicate that even in this kind of activity the somewhat bigger farms are better equipped to make the right kinds of investment.

In one respect recent trends are likely to continue. Industrialization will advance, and both MICs and LICs will increasingly export manufactured goods to one another and to HICs. The abundance of cheap labor will facilitate the transfer of production from countries where labor is scarce and expensive.

As a consequence trade patterns will become more harmonious. Countries that have exported primary products will take over more of the processing and become exporters of semimanufactured goods or even industrial products in their final form. Some LICs will import raw materials from other LICs in order to produce and export manufactures.

This development will answer a question that was raised implictly by the argumentation above concerning agricultural trade. If LICs in densely populated Asia are to import food from more sparsely populated regions, how are they going to pay for it?

The one factor of production these countries have in abundance is labor. Because of advances in education and training the quality of this labor will increase, but it will remain rather cheap for a long time to come because the movement of people out of agriculture will continue.

This in fact means that there are two answers to the question of how to avoid excessive unemployment. One is rural development, gradually raising the level of traditional nonagricultural activities. The other is broadening the modern sector working for exports as well as for the home market. A combination of these two processes will gradually diminish the differences between the two sectors, and a more cohesive society will emerge.

Rural development is called for in all LICs and probably in most MICs, but in the next few decades an expansion of the modern sector is likely to play a larger role in Asia than in Africa because there is an older industrial tradition and a somewhat higher level of education. At the same time the pressure on the land will make it necessary for more people to leave agriculture than can find appropriate occupations in the rural areas without a radical change in the present patterns of development.

Political Development

If there is any general conclusion that can be drawn from the above reasoning about economic and social development, it is that strong factors are at work that threaten to increase disharmony in many national societies. Other factors, including an increasing awareness of the dangers, are working in the opposite direction. The outcome will depend above all on the ability of the political systems, national and international, to devise policies that are based on sufficient understanding of the real problems. These policies must also be based on a willingness on the part of those who are strong to abstain from an abuse of their power. This brings us to the difficult problem of future trends in political development.

Few things are more difficult to evaluate than trends and events in political affairs. On the whole it must be expected that where disharmony prevails, authoritarian regimes are likely to remain in power for a long time to come. Such regimes may also take over in cases in which too many problems remain unsolved for years. The question then is whether the authoritarian regime is working towards the establishment of a more harmonious society, as it seems to have done in such cases as Peru; but this is by no means a general rule.

The growing importance of international economic transactions was stressed in Chapter 7. A corollary of that should be an increasing internationalization of political decision making, or at least an advance in the coordination of national policies. Progress in this direction has been slow and difficult although an elaborate system of international organizations has been established. When governments have difficulties at home, as most governments have today, they cannot easily pay much attention to the international repercussions of the policies for which they are responsible.

We may, however, be entering a phase in which there will be a more important role for the international organizations to play. Until now, bilateral aid from Western industrial countries has dominated the flow of capital and technical assistance to the so-called developing countries, but the new situation in the oil market will unavoidably threaten this flow. If most HICs are to have large deficits in their foreign payments, the temptation to reduce the volume of development assistance will be very strong. At the same time a few oil exporting countries will have enormous surpluses, which they are bound to invest abroad in one way or another. It has already been indicated by some of them that they will make part of this flow of money available to poorer countries in order to counteract the effects of the higher oil prices. They will no doubt be under pressure to do so, since traditionally they belong to the same group of countries within the international system as the poor importers of their oil. Solidarity among the members of this group has been an important part of its philosophy, and therefore the rich oil exporting countries will be under pressure to do something in favor of the other members.

It has been suggested that oil could be sold at low prices to poor countries and at high prices to rich countries, but it is doubtful whether such a system would work, even if the exporting countries could agree on it. How could the oil that is destined for the cheap market always be prevented from finding its way through various channels to the high-priced market? It would be an all too tempting chance to purchase cheaply in the former market and sell high in the latter.

The situation, then, is this: The oil exporting countries have the capital the poor countries need, but they do not have much of the knowledge these countries need even more. On the other hand the HICs have this knowledge, but for some years to come they will not have the capital.

The correct solution of these problems is obviously to combine the knowledge of the HICs with the capital of the oil exporting countries and channel both to the LICs and to some MICs. The obvious instrument for doing this is the system of international organizations centered around the United Nations.

An alternative solution might be for the oil exporting countries to establish their own fund for development assistance; and at least part of the capital may actually be channeled through one or more such funds. Capital, however, is only an instrument for the application of knowledge; these two factors of development must work together.

The world, then, is in a difficult situation, but it has a reservoir consisting of three fundamental elements: there is abundant knowledge in most HICs; abundant capital in some MICs; and abundant labor in most LICs. Will the international organizations be able to bring the three together, or will they miss the opportunity?

The answer may to a large extent depend on the readiness of the leading socialist and nonsocialist countries to cooperate in these matters and to exert an appropriate influence on the countries most directly concerned.

A new development seems to have come about in the relations between the USSR in particular and such nonsocialist countries as the United States, West Germany, and Japan. China has also intensified its relations with non-socialist countries. This development will of course be facilitated if we are on the way to what has been called a convergence of the two types of political systems.

This question has been the subject of a lively debate. To me there is no doubt that the trend is towards convergence, and the analysis undertaken in this book has strengthened this view.

It appeared from the analysis in Chapters 4 through 7 that in those fields where information was available there was no systematic difference between the recent development in socialist and nonsocialist countries. It is also obvious that the nonsocialist countries are much less "capitalistic" than they were 30 or 50 years ago. Capital is subject to public control and taxation. Increasingly it is being replaced by knowledge as the dominant factor of production, but knowledge cannot be nationalized in the same way as land or capital. A knowledge aristocracy has developed, in the USSR as well as in the West. At the same time a decentralization of decision making has taken place in socialist countries. When multinational corporations are allowed to make investments in these countries, forms have to be found that combine some of the elements of the two systems.

Fortunately this dynamic development does not mean that one of the two parties has won an ideological battle and the other has lost. What is happening is that clichés that were formulated in the 19th century, and which reflected the situation at that time, are gradually becoming out of date. Future HICs will be different from both the present socialist and the present nonsocialist societies.

The terms socialist and capitalist are more relevant in the earlier stages of the typical development process. In LICs land is usually the dominant factor of production, but capital is of growing importance. The ownership and the control of these factors are therefore real policy issues; predominantly agrarian societies can choose a more socialist or a more capitalist route on their way towards future types of knowledge societies. This will be discussed in the last section of the present chapter.

LONGER-TERM PROBLEMS

It is hardly possible to say much about trends beyond the end of the present century, and therefore the following considerations are confined to a discussion of some of the major problems that are likely to come up, which policy makers should already have in mind now.

It is obvious that the present type of development, with rapid population growth and still more rapid expansion of many physical activities, cannot continue far into the future. It must be replaced by a different kind of process. This does not necessarily mean that development will be replaced by stagnation; there can be further development of knowledge, of understanding of the world, or of moral attitudes and human relations; that is, more generally, there can be further development of the human personality.

If there is to be a stable world community, however, it will be necessary that the number of people and the volume of certain physical activities be kept at levels that are sustainable in the long run. On the basis of present knowledge it would seem that the 21st century could be a period in which the important but difficult transition to a more stable society really gets underway. This implies that sufficient wisdom will be displayed by those in power. If not, the next century may well be characterized by unrest and human suffering on a large scale.

It would of course be of great interest to know at what level a stabilization of world population might take place and how long this would take. The UN Population Report quoted in the last section contains some projections based on assessments of 1968.[7] These are to be superseded by new (1973) assessments, but it is said in paragraph 70 of the report that the new projections are not expected to differ very substantially from those based on 1968 data.[8] I therefore quote these projections in rounded billions.

	2000	2025	2050	2075
Presently more developed regions	1.4	1.7	1.8	1.9
Presently less developed regions	5.1	7.5	9.4	10.2
Total	6.5	9.2	11.2	12.1

It is indicated in the text[9] that eventually world population might stabilize at about 12.3 billion according to these "medium" assumptions (16 billion according to high assumptions and 9.8 billion according to low assumptions).

If these medium assumptions should prove to be reasonably correct, two conclusions would emerge: First, nearly all the population growth will take place in the less developed regions which roughly correspond to Groups 4 through 7 in the tables of this book. Second, the major part of the increase will take place in the first half of the 21st century. This would imply that population growth would more or less come to a halt around the end of the 21st century.

What, under such assumptions, would be the major development problems during the slowing down in the increase of world population? The nature of the development process would gradually change a great deal. Services would represent an increasing part of total GNP, especially in the richer countries. Still, the pressure on various natural resources might reach dangerous proportions, particularly if the LICs should succeed in catching up with the richer countries.

Let us assume, as an example, that the world's population would be about 12 billion in the year 2100 and that its average income level would be that foreseen for HICs under Assumption 2 in the previous section. In that case the total GNP for the world would be about 8 times its level in the year 2000 according to Assumption 2, or about 30 times its actual level in 1967. This is obviously unrealistic if we think of a gross product of the present type. Even if a large part of this gross produce consisted of services, these speculative figures should be enough to indicate that the development process towards the end of the next century is likely to be something very different from what we know today. Even a modified extrapolation of present trends would be meaningless. A look at some of the major aspects of the development process may help to amplify this argument.

There are two possibilities of overcoming some of the obstacles to further increases in consumption of raw materials. They are substitution and recycling.

To a large extent some raw materials can be substituted for others of great scarcity. In the longer run recycling may, however, become more important. This process is already used for some metals, and since in the very long run mankind must live on its income and not on its capital, future societies should increasingly become recycling communities. An interesting consequence of such a development is that the differences between countries that are rich in deposits of certain ores and countries that are not, should gradually diminish. This is a long-term prospect, though. We may have to go through a rather long period during which those differences will increase.

It should also be remembered that the possibilities of both substitution and recycling are limited, and scarcity of some raw materials of critical importance may raise difficult problems during the next century.

One of the most important questions will be how to develop sources of energy of a more lasting nature than the fossil fuels, which we are rapidly exhausting. Nuclear fusion and solar energy are the two main possibilities. It is essential that they be sufficiently developed in time to prevent an acute energy shortage from putting a brake on the development process. The transition to a more stable society should be smooth: if important bottlenecks appear abruptly they might have serious consequences for the LICs, which will be in a weak position in the competition for scarce resources.

These countries would, by the way, have a comparative advantage in solar energy, since most of them are tropical or subtropical and therefore have more sunshine. Solar energy also has the advantage that it can be utilized in small units at moderate cost.

The environment will be influenced by many of the activities of a growing world population; even climate may be modified in perhaps a dangerous way by increased energy conversion. One of the possibilities is that the icecaps of the polar zones might melt and submerge large inhabited areas.

In general it can be said that the more people are on the earth, and the larger the volume of their activities, the more the situation of the whole biosphere of our planet will be modified. One of the most crucial questions concerning future development is whether enough will be known about such possible modifications before they occur so that appropriate measures can be taken before it is too late.

Food Production

One human activity is of particular importance for the survival of man, namely food production.

World population may reach a level of three times its present size or more during the 21st century. The larger part of mankind has today a nutritional standard that is so low that it must be characterized as unacceptable in a world community marked by human solidarity. The food supply would therefore have to reach much higher levels than at present if we are to achieve a sustainable type of development in a future world society, with 12 billion or more inhabitants.

According to Assumption 2 in the second section of this chapter, food consumption around the year 2000 would represent 38,300 billion primary calories, or more than twice its level in 1967. If a world population of about 12 billion were to have the same nutritional standard as that achieved by HICs, then in the year 2000, according to the same assumption, total food consumption would reach some 140,000 billion primary calories, or nearly ten times its 1967 level.

This, of course, assumes that our descendants will have roughly the same kinds of foods that we have in the richest countries today. One can be sure that this will not be the case in the long run. Fishing cannot be expected to reach ten times its present level; nor can cereals or other crops be expected to yield ten times as much per hectare. It is therefore pretty certain that the patterns of food production will change in a very important way.

This does not mean that world famine is bound to occur during the next century; what it does mean is that in order to prevent a dangerous situation from coming up, a number of very important problems regarding the production and distribution of food must be solved. It is absolutely essential that they be solved before an acute food shortage occurs in large parts of the world. Therefore the nature of these problems must be studied carefully in time, and the time to give increased attention to them is now. During the last few years the trend in food production in the world as a whole has been somewhat disappointing, and as shown in Chapter 5 the nutritional standard in LICs has remained disturbingly low and has even deteriorated in some cases.

There are a number of possibilities. One of the most promising may in the near future be the production of single-cell protein from petroleum, as discussed in the previous section. In fact it should already now be considered how a certain part of the world's oil resources could be reserved for this purpose, since it is at least conceivable that in a few decades the food problem may be more critical than the energy problem.

There are other possibilities of nonagricultural food production, such as the cultivation of algae, the extraction of protein from certain leaves, and even the production of carbohydrate materials from wood. They may become important in the longer run only, and there is no need to discuss them further here. A few remarks are, however, appropriate concerning two possibilities for relying more on plants and less on animals than we do at present.

Since it takes on the average about seven calories of feeding stuff to produce one calorie of animal food, it is obviously an expensive way of getting energy for human work to get food through the animals. If, nevertheless, we do it on an increasing scale, it is because animal protein is particularly valuable as building material for the growth and maintenance of the human body. The various kinds of proteins we get from plants contain less of some critically important amino acids than do the proteins obtained from milk, eggs, and meat. This is why especially poor people in LICs, who can afford very little animal food, are getting insufficient nutrition. It is even considered important for the development of the brain, that children get more and better protein during the first years after weaning. It is therefore a positive feature of recent development that animal food is playing an increasing role, as shown in Table 5.10.

There is, however, a risk that we may have to move backwards again in this respect as the world population grows. About two-thirds of all primary calories produced are now used as feed for animals; evidently more people could be fed if some of these calories were used directly as human food.

Two kinds of research are going on that may help us to release more calories for direct human consumption without a serious deterioration of the nutritional standard. Modern methods of feeding aim at reducing the rates of conversion, so that the same amount of animal food can be obtained by smaller inputs of feeding stuffs; even more important is the work on increasing the quantities of protein contained in various plants and in particular increasing the amounts of some of the critically important amino acids in various kinds of plant protein. We may therefore, if it should be necessary, be able to reduce the stock of various domestic animals and yet get valuable nutrition. It would be important in such a case to avoid a serious reduction of the number of ruminants, which are able to utilize straw and other inferior elements of plants to a rather large extent, which hogs and poultry cannot do.

The question remains, however, whether people in the richer countries would go on eating large quantities of animal food even if the world situation in general should indicate that a substantial reduction of livestock were desirable. If food is becoming scarce it will also become expensive, and that should reduce effective demand. But does this mean that rich people will be content with a somewhat more modest diet, or will the result be that poor people will be forced to reduce a nutritional standard that is already too low?

A similar question can be asked about possible shortages of energy or of certain important raw materials. This forces us to consider the future of the really poor societies, which in all likelihood will be the most important development problem in the 21st century.

The Development Process

It should appear from the above analysis that even if the most optimistic of the two assumptions should prove realistic, the gap between LICs and MICs is bound to widen during the next few decades. If economic expansion in the world as a whole should slow down considerably during the next century, will the present LICs ever be able to catch up with the richer countries? If not, can serious unrest and violence on a large scale be avoided?

It is hardly possible today to give a clear answer to any of these crucial questions. What follows is therefore only an attempt to draw up an outline of the complex of problems that will come up. Combined efforts by students of many disciplines will be needed to give us a fuller understanding, and governments will have to proceed by trial and error through a long period, because too little is known about the nature of the transition to a different kind of development, which it is increasingly being felt that we will have to go through.

The first thing to underline is how important it is to see the development of rich and of poor countries as integral parts of one development process. The greatest risk during the transition is perhaps that shortages of various kinds will give countries that are in a strong position more power than the weaker nations in the competition for resources. Today the oil-producing countries, which are rich in certain mineral resources, may be in a similar position, but in the long run the greatest advantages may accrue to the richer nations because they have the most efficient productive machinery. Above all they possess by far the largest part of the great stock of knowledge, which contains the only clue we may have to the difficult problems concerning energy, food production, scarcity of some raw materials, and the establishment of a true international monetary system, as well as a certain control of capital movements and multinational corporations.

The one great asset of the poorest countries is their abundant labor force. Their population is growing too fast, but since that cannot be avoided for some time to come, the many hands that will result should be put to work. Not only can they be used to provide better housing and sanitary installations in their own societies, but they can also take over an increasing part of the world's industrial production. I should not omit that capital shortage in the presently rich countries, as well as the need to recycle more and more materials, will increase the interest in relatively labor intensive processes, such as sorting out what is useful in what would otherwise be waste. The rising standard of education in the present LICs should facilitate transfers of production to them.

The labor shortage in the present HICs should work in the same direction. Whether this shortage will continue, as it may well do, is one of the problems of the next century. These countries seem bound to have many internal problems in the foreseeable future. Their capital surplus will be transformed into a large deficit for perhaps many years to come, and this may counteract the tendency to have more and more expensive labor-saving machinery; the fight against inflation may also put a brake on such investment. It will not be easy to prevent the public sector from absorbing an increasing part of the labor force in countries in which a long period of parliamentary democracy has created intense competition between political parties, tempting them to offer more and more to the public.

One of the problems of the future will be how international cooperation will develop in a world where so many countries have difficult internal problems. As mentioned in the second section of this chapter, the main problem of the next few decades may be how to combine the knowledge surplus of the HICs and the capital surplus of some oil exporting countries, with the labor surplus of the LICs. There may be similar problems to cope with in later phases of the transition to a stabler world society. It will also be necessary to establish a more stable international monetary system; this will imply a need for cooperation between countries regarding control of capital movements and of some of the operations of multinational corporations.

These problems will be dealt with in the last section of this chapter as part of a general discussion of some policy issues related to the development process.

POLICY ISSUES

The problems discussed below are all related to policies that might be pursued during the next few years. It is, however, of the greatest importance that they be pursued in view of both the medium-term and the long-term problems discussed in the two preceding sections. Nobody knows exactly how great the risks are of dangerous imbalances some decades further ahead, but there should be no doubt that much can be done during the remainder of the present century to reduce these risks. It so happens that some of the measures we can take to prepare for the next century will also be helpful during the next two or three decades.

I have found it useful to group the following considerations under four headings. There is of course much overlapping among the various categories of problems, but more light can be thrown on some of them if they are looked at from more than one angle.

The Need for Research

It is already of the highest importance that research be undertaken on both long-term and medium-term problems. It may take many years to find out what are the possibilities as well as the risks concerning productive utilization of nuclear fusion, solar energy, or the protein contained in leaves of various plants. Therefore, intensive work should be done on these and other long-term problems from now on.

At the same time, there are urgent problems concerning alternative energy resources and alternative methods of production, and of house construction with a view to saving energy, and oil in particular. No less urgent are the problems created by the changes in the flows of capital that will result from the larger sums paid for oil from many importers to a few exporters. In these fields, too, careful analysis is needed before policy decisions are made.

Politicians are bound to be preoccupied by these urgent problems. It is therefore the responsibility of the international scientific community, to see to it that the long-term problems are not forgotten. The task is complicated by the fact that the resources allocated to scientific work may be more limited than one would wish. There will therefore be a need to develop an international science policy. Its purpose will be to define priorities and to find out who can do what, and how wasteful duplication of work can be avoided.

This will not be an easy task, but certain elements of such a policy do exist already. National science policies are being developed in many countries, and OECD has done pioneering work in this field.[10] The United Nations has done useful work on research concerning problems related specifically to development.[11] Furthermore, certain organizations within the scientific community itself are trying to coordinate the work of a number of research institutions.

It is particularly important to organize research on alternative ways of solving the problems related to the consumption and production of energy and of food, both long-term and short-term. In both cases new technologies should be developed in time, so that periods of acute shortage can be avoided.

Concerning energy there is one particular aspect of the problem to which too little attention may have been paid until now. If coal and nuclear energy are to play an increasing role because of a shortage of oil, the tendency will be to establish big units in which the energy may be used directly or transformed into electricity. This will be sufficient for those consumers, including industry and railways, who can be linked to a grid, but what will happen to mobile units like motor cars, tractors, ships, and airplanes?

In some countries there may be too many motor cars and too much air transport that is only of secondary importance. But it is of great importance for the maintenance of cohesive national and international communities, that such mobile units function on a rather large scale. The further development of LICs may be hampered seriously if they cannot.

Electric motor cars do exist, but they have so far had only a narrow range of action. Work is being done on other devices. Further work in this field should be given high priority.

Another important subject of high priority is of course research on the ecological consequences of human activities. There has been a certain anxiety on the part of some MICs and LICs who fear that too much concern about the environment may prevent them from developing a modern industry. It is therefore necessary to stress that the ecological problems of, say, tropical LICs are to a large extent different from those of temperate-zone HICs. At the same time it is worth mentioning that the present LICs have a chance to avoid some of the mistakes made by those countries who were pioneers in industrial development.

Of particular importance in this respect is a careful analysis of the ecological consequences of an intensive use of fertilizers and pesticides in agriculture. There is already much concern in some HICs about the ensuing pollution of rivers and lakes and, more importantly, of the food produced.

An interesting symptom of this fear is a movement among farmers and horticulturists, making propaganda for the production of nonpolluted foods. Experiments are being made in which chemical fertilizers are being replaced by manure and by compost. This is a rather labor intensive technique, but although less can be produced in this way than by ordinary modern methods it must be admitted that it is a symbol of the recycling society that is being so heatedly discussed at the moment.

We may have to decide whether beyond certain limits more food should be produced on the same land, if the side effect is bound to be a critical increase in pollution. We need more research to guide us in such questions. It is worth noting that these problems will be different in tropical LICs from what they are in HICs in the temperate zone.

It is tempting to conclude that we need much more research than we can possibly have, because both human and material resources are limited. This is why we need to define priorities through an international science policy for development.

Problems of Low Income Countries

How can LICs get out of the extreme poverty from which a large part of their population suffers because of increasing unemployment and the further fragmentation of small agricultural holdings? To this question two answers have been proposed in recent years: Rural development and appropriate technology. A combination of these two kinds of innovation should counteract an excessive rural-urban migration and create the basis for a socially more balanced development of the whole society.

By rural development is understood a mixed policy aimed at improving agricultural techniques and establishing small-scale industries in the rural areas, to process the products of farming and to supply the farmers with consumer goods and with various means of production. In this way more employment is created, the standard of living in the countryside should improve somewhat, and it would be less attractive to go to the cities in search of a future that may prove to be more difficult than expected by some of the young people.

Both in agriculture and in the rural industries referred to, techniques should be appropriate. What this means may vary much from one place to another. The use of expensive and sophisticated machinery imported from abroad should be avoided. To the extent possible, materials existing in the country should be used. Above all, techniques should be labor intensive, using much labor and little capital.

There is much truth in these ideas. They would give to the development process some of the continuity it has shown in countries that have been in the oft-mentioned main stream of human progress for centuries. I do think, however, that a more complex system of policies is called for in order to ensure that development will be both continuous and progressive, also in the longer run. One might consider four components of such an integrated policy mix:

1. There should certainly be rural development, with appropriate technology as described above. Research is needed to find out what kinds of technology are appropriate in the country or regions in question. Practical experiments will be an important part of this research. Research institutes do exist in this field; they should cooperate closely with field workers in a system of extension services for agriculture and for industry. It would

therefore be a mixture of an academic exercise and of trial and error in the workshops.

2. At the same time an effort should be made to broaden the modern sector. LICs should profit from the fact that there is a labor shortage in the rich countries. Multinational corporations can be helpful by making investments in LICs and producing there for the national market and for exports, but their subsidiaries should not be allowed to become enclaves in the economy and society of the LIC. This means that LICs should have a policy concerning their relations with multinational corporations. Hopefully, they will soon be able to formulate a coherent policy in this field through exchange of experience and through consultation with international organizations and experts and practitioners from more industrialized countries.

It might be part of such a policy that the enterprise in question will employ and train an appropriate number of nationals of the country, apply techniques that are relatively labor intensive, utilize materials from the country, and undertake research there. It may also be made a condition that the enterprise be a joint venture, part of the capital belonging to nationals or to the government of the LIC. In this way foreign subsidiaries will gradually become more integrated in the national economy. If a progressive rural development is taking place at the same time, the difference between the modern and the traditional sector will be reduced and a more cohesive society will emerge.

3. A third element in a coherent policy should be the establishment of a system of appropriate education. As stressed in Chapter 5 there has been too much imitation of Western educational systems. Education should be so devised that the adaptive innovation discussed in Chapter 3 can become a two-way traffic. Appropriate technology should be adapted to the situation of the country in question, yet it will be something new, aimed at raising the level of the traditional sector progressively. People should therefore on their part be adapted to these new tasks. Vocational training should be part of both primary and secondary education. Even more important, perhaps, is the establishment of a work-oriented system of adult education. There are more than 700 million illiterate adults in LICs today, as shown in Table 5.23, and their numbers are still growing slowly. Not only is there a danger of a serious generation gap between illiterate parents and children who have gone to school, but it is also important that the present generation of adults be prepared for some of the jobs of a changing society. Also, if democratic systems of government are going to work, the electorate must know something about at least some of the new features of its national society and its relations with the outside world.

It will also be the task of an appropriate system of education to train field workers of the extension service in agriculture and industry, and of course to train teachers for the future-work oriented primary and secondary schools. These teachers may then become responsible for adult education too.

Universities in LICs will often be weak for obvious reasons, but if they concentrate on research and higher education designed for the society to which they belong, they may gradually become able to counteract the brain drain. Students may well find that there are fascinating tasks in their own country, including the importation of foreign knowledge and its adaptation to a society about which they know more than do foreign scientists and technicians.

The importance of such a system of appropriate education can hardly be overestimated. To develop a country means, more than anything else, to develop its people. One talks about nation-building in the newly independent states; nothing is more suited to the building of a nation that educating its people in ways that are adapted to the nature of the country and the society they are going to be responsible for.

4. There remains the difficult problem of land reform. In countries where agricultural holdings are too big or too small, no harmonious rural development is possible. But appropriate land reform means something very different in these two cases. In countries with big estates a splitting up of these into medium-sized farms may be appropriate. Landless laborers can then become farmers. Where very small farms prevail in a densely populated country, the danger is rather that further fragmentation will create units that are insufficient as a living place for a family and ill suited for the application of modern techniques. In such countries amalgamation or collectivization will be the appropriate type of land reform.

In both cases there will often be resistance from those who own the land, whether they be large-scale farmers or absentee landlords. If small farmers own the land they cultivate it may also be difficult to get agreement on cooperative farming on a voluntary basis. How can one be sure that each farmer will get an appropriate part of the output?

This can be a painful dilemma, but there is a grave risk that the Green Revolution in Asia will benefit the bigger farmers to such an extent that we get a new class of landlords with mechanized farms. The small farmers will not be able to compete with them, and the landless laborers will find it increasingly difficult to get jobs.

The best solution may therefore be expropriation in both cases. Governments may have to take over land from the big estates in the first type of country and distribute it to a new class of farmers. In the other type of country governments may be forced to take over the land of the small farmers and then organize collective farming. Since this will require less labor than did the tiny farms, there will be an occasion for the establishment of agro-allied and other industries in the rural areas in order to provide employment and further a broader type of development. This is more or less what China has done, although in this case the land was expropriated from bigger landowners.

If these remarks about land reform are combined with what was said above, concerning the role of government in its relations with subsidiaries of foreign corporations, light is thrown on a rather fundamental problem. It may be possible for many of the present LICs to bypass the feudal and capitalist phases other countries have gone through on their way to the modern industrial society of typical HICs. This will require that governments play a rather important role in the transition from predominantly agrarian societies to the future type of mixed society, the nature of which we can only have vague and preliminary views about today. As I have stressed in other parts of this book, the terms capitalist and socialist are gradually losing their meaning with respect to present or future knowledge societies, but are more meaningful in the earlier phases of the typical development process, in which land and the capital of an emerging industry are dominant factors. The conclusion to draw from the above argument is therefore that it will probably be appropriate for many LICs to follow a relatively socialistic route from their present types of societies to the unknown future types.

In doing so they should leave room for initiative and decentralized decision making, but they would do well to prevent the accumulation of large amounts of land and capital in the hands of persons who are too powerful in their relations with poor workers or peasants. Governments should control the development process more than it was necessary, or possible, at similar stages of the development of countries where the process has been longer and more continuous.

Problems of Middle Income Countries and High Income Countries

It will appear from the analysis in this book that on the whole MICs have experienced both rapid economic growth and rapid social transformation in recent years. The differences between these countries and the HICs are therefore diminishing and this means that increasingly the two groups will have to face the same types of policy problems.

This must of course be taken with a grain of salt. The MICs are a very mixed group of countries, and many of them are still rather close to the LICs in various respects. The similarities between Latin America and Africa have been stressed in some of the preceding chapters. In some cases MICs will undoubtedly have to face some problems that are characteristic of HICs, at the same time that they share other problems with the LICs.

It should be sufficient to outline below some of the more important problems related to the further development of HICs. Combined with those of the LICs described above, they represent a spectrum within which some of the most topical problems of MICs should also be covered.

As stressed in a previous section, many of the difficulties of modern industrial societies stem from the fact that knowledge has been developing in a disharmonious way. This is certainly the case regarding the environmental problems. We have learned how to increase the output of agriculture by means of fertilizers and pesticides, but we have not learned how to tackle the problems created by the ensuing pollution of rivers, lakes, and foodstuffs. We have learned how to fight against many kinds of disease, but often the medicines used have harmful side effects that were not foreseen. The noise and the pollution of the air created by automobiles and airplanes are other examples of negative side effects of innovations that were carried through because of the positive effects they also have.

These are typical examples of a "development disease." Difficulties arise because structural changes in human society take place in a disharmonious way. It will increasingly become necessary to postpone the application of new knowledge until research has created sufficient supplementary knowledge about the difficulties it might create and about how to tackle the problems involved. Nuclear fission is a case in point, and at the same time demonstrates how difficult it may be to get agreement. How great are the dangers? How do they compare with the advantages? Unfortunately there will in most cases be no common unit in which dangers and advantages can be measured.

If the rich countries are to have steadily increasing levels of income, many environmental problems are likely to come up. It is therefore essential that procedures be worked out to ensure that undue risks are avoided. If there is any general field where it is true that prevention is better than cure, it is the preservation of an acceptable environment.

The accelerating inflation in many HICs is another development disease. It did not exist in anything like the same proportions in earlier periods. This is not the place for a lengthy discussion of economic policy, but a discussion of recent inflation is appropriate, to the extent that it results from recent development; that is, from structural change in our societies. The trouble is that if inflation results from the development process itself it is not easy to counteract it.

In fact modern inflation does result from the development of recent decades in three respects. First, investment represents an increasing part of the GNP in modern industrial societies. In contrast to consumption investment, it can be subject to important fluctuations. The production of butter must follow demand, but there have been ups and downs in investment in ships, houses, and machinery. These fluctuations are cumulative up to a point: an increase in investment stimulates the whole economy and thereby the demand for still more investment.

Similarly, a downward movement is cumulative until a certain point. The great depression of the 1930s was a drastic example of this, and as a reaction all countries pushed demand in the years after World War II. One of the results of this has been cumulative inflation.

The second respect in which modern inflation results from development has been the increasing tendency for all kinds of professional groups to organize and to press for higher incomes. It is very difficult for democratic governments to resist such pressure.

The third factor, finally, is the rapid increase in trade and communication between countries resulting from modern technical development. This means that inflation spreads very easily from one country to another.

In a way, the recent violent increase of oil prices is an example of the second of the three factors mentioned above. The oil-producing countries are one of the many pressure groups created by recent development. There may be more such international pressure groups in the future.

Is there any cure for the disease of inflation, to the extent it is a byproduct of the development process? I think there is. It is a well-known fact that some diseases produce an antidote that after a while counteracts the disease. In social affairs the "awareness" mentioned several times in this book is such an antidote: if enough people become aware that something is wrong, there will be a new motivation to counteract it.

One of the latest results of the Egalitarian Revolution is the demand for participation of employees in the decisions of enterprises. In some countries this includes the demand to own part of the capital of the enterprise in one form or another.

If workers have representatives on the board of a corporation and own part of the stock, they will become aware that it is not in their interest to increase wages to an extent that endangers the survival or the continued expansion of the enterprise.

Another product of modern development is the "knowledge aristocracy" I have mentioned earlier in this book. The importance of knowledge has strengthened the position of those who have a great deal of it, and sometimes people with higher education lead the race for higher incomes, thus pushing inflation. In this case the antidote has been a widespread desire to have higher education, and there is now overproduction in several lines of study in various countries. This increase in supply is beginning to diminish the strength of the knowledge aristocracy.

In a more general way the antidote against inflation may be an awareness that if all pressure groups get a certain increase in their nominal incomes nobody gets anything in terms of real income.

There is by no means any guarantee that awareness will cure a certain social disease in time, but in a period of rapid change it is an important policy issue to create sufficient awareness not only of existing difficulties but also of difficulties that may come up on the foreseeable future.

One such difficulty may be the risk of unemployment during the slowing down of rapid economic expansion that can be expected in most HICs in the decades to come. This may be precipitated by the balance of payments difficulties that these countries will have because of the increase in oil prices.

The high rates of investment referred to above are closely linked to rapid economic growth. Many people have been employed because there was a demand for such growth production as more houses, more hospitals, more cars and roads, and more perfect 'machinery. If we are now moving towards zero population growth and slower economic development, many of these jobs will become redundant, and a different kind of policy will be required.

There is no reason why there should be more unemployment in a society without economic growth than in an expanding economy. If there is less investment, more workers can produce consumer goods and services. It will, however, be necessary for a great many people to change jobs, maybe several times during their working years. Retraining should therefore be part of the future system of education.

One consequence of a slowing down may be that the large cities will stop growing; in fact, a certain de-urbanization might well become appropriate. The trend in agriculture is towards fewer and larger farms. Many villages may virtually disappear. There will therefore be ample space in the rural areas. Why should people go on living in crowded urban agglomerations if the race for larger shares of an expanding national product is beginning to slow down? The big cities have been a symptom of industrial expansion.

The above considerations reflect something that may be an essential feature of future societies. It was stressed in the previous section that a slowing down of physical expansion need not mean that development will have to stop. What it means is that a life style will be developed that is very different from the one that has characterized the period of rapid expansion.

There are good reasons for beginning to prepare for such a different type of development now. Societies in various parts of the world have developed different kinds of life styles during earlier phases of history. A new life style in the presently highly industrialized societies would be identical with none of them, although there might be common features. It would be based on our present knowledge about the world, further extended and widened, but it would probably make people less dependent on material progress. The transition to such a life style will not be easy, but more satisfaction may result when it is achieved.

The Need for International Cooperation

There are two problems that will dominate the international scene in the years to come. One is the need to maintain peace or at least to avoid major hostilities. The other is the urgent question referred to in an earlier section of this chapter: How can we bring the surplus capital of oil-producing countries, the surplus knowledge of HICs, and the surplus labor of LICs together?

The tension between the USSR and Western HICs has been diminishing in recent years, and the trend towards convergence between the two systems should enhance this development. This new development may give rise to progress in the discussions about disarmament. An obstacle seems to be disagreement between the two major parties about the relative proportions by which their respective forces in Europe should be reduced, and substantial steps forward can perhaps not be taken in the near future. A more fundamental problem, however, is how the two parties can cooperate in cases of conflict in various places, since there seems to be no doubt that both are aware of the common interest they have in preventing tensions from spreading. At the same time economic cooperation between them seems to be developing to some extent, and the present stage of development regarding energy should favor this, since the USSR has considerable resources of fossil fuels.

The enormous changes in the world's capital markets that will result from the increase of oil prices requires urgent consideration of their consequences. The International Monetary Fund has offered to make special quotas of its credit facilities available to those countries that are hit by the effects of the oil crisis, and that may be a useful short term measure.

Concerning the long-term problems, it is important to stress that the real resources of the world have not become smaller because energy has become more expensive. In fact a beneficial consequence will be that rich countries will be induced to reduce their consumption of energy for purposes of minor importance, and more oil will be spared for the years we will have to wait until alternative sources of energy have been developed.

It is important that bilateral technical assistance programs of HICs should not be diminished. Assistance in the form of loans could be channeled through international organizations to a higher degree than before, as discussed below, but bilateral programs of technical assistance are able to mobilize some intellectual resources in HICs that might not otherwise be utilized. In many HICs a number of scientists and technicians have worked for years in MICs or LICs or at home on problems related to development, and these persons will usually be motivated for further work in this field. Often they are more easily engaged by their own country, where they are known, than by an international organization.

It is equally important that research done in HICs on problems related to the development of poorer countries be continued. Balance of payments difficulties may force HICs to reduce the resources they allocate to various tasks, but the mobilization of the knowledge regarding development that they possess should not be hindered.

An encouraging new development has started in the field of technical assistance in recent years. A number of MICs, and LICs such as China, India, and Taiwan, have become donors. This is particularly important because such countries often have experience that is more relevant than that of the richer countries. A further development of this kind of aid should be discussed in the UN family of organizations. An extension might be possible if it were financed by countries that are more wealthy.

The important question that has come up in respect to the transfer of knowledge is how to make sure that the knowledge that exists in rich or poor countries that will now have financial difficulties because of the oil crisis will nevertheless be made available. A tripartite agreement might be made between countries that have such available knowledge, oil exporting countries who have the available capital, and appropriate parts of the United Nations systems of organizations. Regional development banks can also be given a role in such arrangements.

In fact, funds for the financing of technical assistance ought to be given as grants. The best solution might be to establish a special fund based on voluntary contributions from countries that are prepared to make such an effort.

There is another purpose for which grants will also be highly desirable for some years to come. More fertilizers are needed to increase agricultural production in LICs, but they will become more expensive because of the increased oil prices. It is hardly possible to operate a system in which some countries can buy fertilizers at a lower price than others, but if LICs could get subsidies for this special purpose they would be able to buy in the ordinary market.

Many other problems regarding international cooperation will come up for discussion during the next few years. There is the question of further reductions in trade barriers, which is now the subject of negotiations in GATT, and the need for a reform of the international monetary system and for some control of international capital movements is becoming more urgent, but also more difficult to resolve, because of the new situation in the oil market. These questions are of a too specific nature to be taken up in this book about the development process.

It is, however, appropriate to conclude by stressing that anything done in these fields should be so designed that it will contribute to a more harmonious development process, and especially more favorable than at present for the poorest countries.

NOTES

1. Amory Lovins, *World Energy Strategies* (London: Earth Resources Research, 1973), p. 49.

2. Report on the Second Inquiry among Governments on Population and Development, E/CH9/303 (New York: the UN, 1974).

3. *FAO Production Yearbook 1971* (Rome: Food and Agricultural Organization).

4. *FAO, Provisional Indicative World Plan*, Vol. I (Rome: FAO, 1969), Table 8.

5. *FAO Production Yearbook 1971* (Rome: Food and Agricultural Organization).

6. Ibid.

7. World Population Conference, op. cit., Paragraphs 84-85.

8. Ibid., Paragraph 70.

9. Ibid., p. 28.

10. OECD, *Science, Growth and Society, a New Perspective* (Paris: OECD, 1971).

11. United Nations, *World Plan of Action for the Application of Science and Technology to Development* (New York: the UN, 1971).

ANNEX

ABOUT THE TABLES

As a matter of principle the tables in this book have been based on statistical publications by international organizations belonging to the United Nations System of Organizations. This should give a certain guarantee that the statistics included are considered reasonably good. Furthermore they are made comparable among countries.

To the extent possible the tables cover the 122 countries about which basic information is contained in the *World Bank Atlas*. These are all the countries that had more than a million inhabitants in 1967. Taken together they represent between 98 and 99 percent of the world's population.

In the *World Bank Atlas* the figures for net material product of the socialist countries are recalculated in such a way that they correspond to gross national product (GNP) for other countries, as in Table A.1.

The countries are grouped in seven groups according to their income levels (GNP per capita), as shown in Table A.1 and Table 4.1. Group averages are calculated by weighing the countries according to their population and GNP in 1967.

The three main categories of countries used in some tables are as follows:

	Groups
High income countries (HICs)	1-2
Medium income countries (MICs)	3-5
Low income countries (LICs)	6-7

Where it is found useful for the analysis, the same subject is presented in two tables, one based on the seven income groups, the other based on the three main categories, combined with an arrangement of the countries according to the regions to which they belong. In order to make this possible, four of the 122 countries are excluded from the tables based on categories and regions. The four countries are Puerto Rico, Israel, Bolivia, and Haiti. Together they represent less than .5 percent of the total population. By excluding them the following simplifications are obtained:

1. All HICs belong to one of the two first regions presented in Table 4.2, namely (1) North America and Oceania (United States, Canada, Australia and New Zealand); and (2) Europe (meaning virtually all of Western Europe).
2. All Latin American countries are MICs. Therefore MICs can be arranged as shown in Table 4.2.
3. All LICs belong to Asia or Africa.

In this way it has been possible to combine the regional comparisons used in much of the literature about development with the comparisons between income groups that are considered essential in this book.

In those tables where figures have not been available for all 122 countries, it is indicated how many countries are covered, as well as their population in 1967.

In all of the tables, "dollars" means U.S. dollars.

The two "assumptions" underlying the tables contained in Chapter 9 are based on the following observations:

Population. In Table 4.2 it was only possible to give the birth and death rates for part of the MICs and for a small part of the LICs, because information for the year 1960 was not available for other countries in these categories.

For the year 1970 information is available for 118 countries, leaving 6, which represent less than one percent of the total population. The following comparisons between population growth rates can therefore be made:

	1960-70 (Table 4.2)	Natural Increase 1970	1967-2000 Assumption 1	2
HICs	1.0	0.65	0.6	0.3
MICs	1.9	1.80	1.7	1.5
LICs	2.3	2.30	2.4	2.2
Total	2.0	1.9	2.0	1.8

Assumption 1 implies that the downward trends for the HICs will come to a halt, while Assumption 2 implies that it will continue. For MICs the two assumptions represent a modest and a more important continuation of a reduction that may be about to start. For the LICs, finally, Assumption 1 corresponds to the conclusions drawn from the tables in Chapter 6, that population growth is becoming faster in the lowest income groups of countries, while Assumption 2 would imply that the reduction to be expected later would already become rather important before the end of the century.

GNP. Even if growth rates are defined as being reduced, total GNP would be more than four and a half times its 1967 volume in the year 2000 according to Assumption 1, and the level according to Assumption 2 would not be much below four times the 1967 level.

Relatively, the reduction is rather sharp for HICs in both cases, and more modest for MICs. As indicated in Chapter 9, the HICs will be influenced negatively by he increased oil prices, both directly and indirectly. For the MICs the effects will be mixed. Six oil exporting countries are MICs, and their growth rates should increase drastically. On the other hand, Japan will be influenced negatively more than most HICs. The USSR, the biggest MIC, is for the moment a surplus country for oil on a small scale, and it has considerable reserves of coal. On the average, therefore, MICs are better placed concerning

TABLE A.1

Population and GNP of 122 Countries, 1960-1970

	Population 1967 (millions)	GNP 1967 (billions of dollars)	GNP per Capita 1967 (dollars)	Annual Growth 1960-70 (percent) Population	GNP	GNP per Capita
Group 1	306.6	955.5	3,120	1.2	4.6	3.4
United States	199.1	730.7	3,670	1.3	4.5	3.2
Sweden	7.9	19.8	2,500	.7	4.1	3.4
Canada	20.4	48.6	2,380	1.8	4.7	2.8
Switzerland	6.1	14.1	2,310	1.7	4.3	2.6
Australia	11.8	23.2	1,970	2.0	5.0	2.9
Denmark	4.8	9.4	1,950	.7	4.4	3.7
France	49.9	97.3	1,950	1.1	6.0	4.8
New Zealand	2.8	5.3	1,890	1.8	3.8	2.0
Norway	3.8	7.1	1,860	.8	4.8	4.0
Group 2	238.4	354.3	1,490	.8	4.3	3.5
West Germany	59.9	104.8	1,750	1.0	4.7	3.7
Belgium	9.6	16.7	1,740	.6	4.1	3.5
United Kingdom	55.1	93.7	1,700	.7	2.5	1.8
Finland	4.7	7.8	1,660	.7	4.6	3.9
Netherlands	12.6	19.2	1,520	1.3	4.4	3.1
East Germany	17.1	22.2	1,300	−0.1	4.0	4.1
Austria	7.3	8.8	1,210	.5	4.4	3.9
Puerto Rico	2.7	3.3	1,210	3.3	7.8	6.0
Israel	2.7	3.2	1,200	3.3	8.8	5.3
Italy	52.4	58.7	1,120	.8	5.5	4.7
Czechoslovakia	14.3	15.9	1,110	.6	4.5	3.9
Group 3	443.8	413.9	930	1.2	7.8	6.5
Japan	99.9	99.9	1,000	1.0	11.1	10.0
USSR	235.5	228.4	970	1.3	7.0	5.6
Ireland	2.9	2.6	910	.3	3.8	3.5
Hungary	10.2	9.2	900	.3	5.8	5.5
Venezuela	9.4	8.3	880	3.5	6.1	2.5
Argentina	23.3	18.6	800	1.6	4.2	2.6
Trinidad and Tobago	1.0	.8	790	2.5	6.4	3.8
Poland	31.9	24.9	780	1.0	6.2	5.1
Libya	1.7	1.2	720	3.7	26.2	21.7

	Population 1967 (millions)	GNP 1967 (billions of dollars)	GNP per Capita 1967 (dollars)	Annual Growth 1960-70 (percent) Population	GNP	GNP per Capita
Romania	19.3	13.9	720	.9	8.5	7.5
Greece	8.7	6.1	700	.7	6.9	6.2
Group 4	160.9	89.2	550	2.2	6.7	4.4
Bulgaria	8.3	5.7	690	.8	7.6	6.7
Spain	32.1	21.8	680	.9	7.5	6.5
Hong Kong	3.8	2.4	620	2.9	11.9	8.7
Singapore	2.0	1.2	600	2.4	7.0	4.5
South Africa	19.3	11.4	590	2.3	6.2	3.8
Panama	1.3	.7	550	3.3	8.3	4.8
Uruguay	2.8	1.5	550	1.3	.5	− .8
Yugoslavia	19.9	10.5	530	1.1	5.8	4.6
Lebanon	2.5	1.3	520	2.5	4.7	2.1
Mexico	45.7	22.4	490	3.5	7.0	3.4
Chile	9.1	4.3	470	2.5	4.2	1.7
Jamaica	1.9	.9	460	1.5	4.5	3.0
Portugal	9.4	3.9	420	.9	5.8	4.9
Costa Rica	1.6	.7	410	3.3	6.3	2.9
Mongolia	1.2	.5	410	3.1	4.1	1.0
Group 5	299.3	80.0	270	2.9	5.9	2.9
Nicaragua	1.8	.6	360	3.5	6.4	2.8
Peru	12.4	4.3	350	3.1	5.1	1.9
Saudi Arabia	7.0	2.5	350	1.7	8.9	7.1
Cuba	8.0	2.6	330	2.5	− .8	−3.2
Albania	2.0	.6	320	2.9	7.9	4.9
Guatemala	4.7	1.5	310	3.1	5.1	1.9
Colombia	19.2	5.8	300	3.2	4.7	1.5
Malaysia	10.1	2.9	290	3.0	6.9	3.8
Turkey	32.7	9.5	290	2.5	6.0	3.4
Iran	26.3	7.4	280	3.0	8.0	4.9
El Salvador	3.2	.9	270	3.7	5.7	1.9
Dominican Republic	3.9	1.0	260	3.0	3.4	.4
Algeria	12.5	3.1	250	2.4	−1.2	−3.5
Brazil	85.7	21.4	250	3.2	4.6	1.4

(continued)

Table A.1, cont.

	Population 1967 (millions)	GNP 1967 (billions of dollars)	GNP per Capita 1967 (dollars)	Annual Growth 1960-70 (percent) Population	GNP	GNP per Capita
Taiwan	13.1	3.3	250	3.0	9.5	6.3
Jordan	2.0	.5	250	3.2	8.1	4.7
Honduras	2.4	.6	240	3.4	4.5	1.1
Iraq	8.4	1.9	230	3.5	6.6	3.0
Ivory Coast	4.0	.9	230	2.8	7.6	4.7
North Korea	12.7	2.9	230	2.6	8.7	5.9
Rhodesia	4.5	1.0	230	3.2	3.6	.4
Paraguay	2.2	.5	220	3.1	4.1	1.0
Ecuador	5.5	1.2	210	3.4	4.6	1.2
Tunisia	4.6	1.0	210	3.0	5.2	2.1
Ghana	8.1	1.6	200	2.5	2.5	.0
Papua and New Guinia	2.3	.5	200	2.4	4.4	2.0
Group 6	375.6	50.4	130	2.5	5.2	2.6
Angola	5.3	1.0	190	1.3	2.7	1.4
Liberia	1.1	.2	190	2.8	4.1	1.3
Morocco	14.1	2.7	190	2.9	6.4	3.4
Senegal	3.7	.7	190	2.2	2.1	− .1
Mozambique	7.1	1.3	180	1.8	5.2	3.3
Philippines	34.7	6.2	180	3.1	5.1	1.9
Syria	5.6	1.0	180	2.8	7.6	4.7
Zambia	3.9	.7	180	2.6	8.1	5.4
Bolivia	3.8	.6	170	2.6	5.1	2.4
Sri Lanka	11.7	1.9	160	2.4	4.6	2.1
South Korea	29.8	4.8	160	2.6	9.2	6.4
Egypt	30.9	4.9	160	2.5	3.7	1.2
Sierra Leone	2.4	.3	140	2.0	3.2	1.2
Cambodia	6.4	.8	130	3.3	3.8	.5
Cameroon	5.5	.7	130	2.1	4.1	2.0
Mauritania	1.1	.1	130	2.2	6.9	4.6
South Yemen	1.3	.2	130	2.2	−2.5	−4.6
Thailand	32.7	4.3	130	3.1	7.9	4.7
Central African Republic	1.5	.2	120	2.4	2.4	.0

	Population 1967 (millions)	GNP 1967 (billions of dollars)	GNP per Capita 1967 (dollars)	Annual Growth 1960-70 (percent) Population	GNP	GNP per Capita
Kenya	9.9	1.2	120	3.1	4.6	1.5
South Vietnam	17.0	2.0	120	2.7	4.5	1.8
Indonesia	110.1	11.0	100	2.4	3.2	.8
Malagasy Republic	6.4	.6	100	2.4	2.4	.0
Togo	1.7	.2	100	2.6	2.6	.0
Uganda	7.9	.8	100	3.0	4.8	1.7
North Vietnam	20.1	2.0	100	3.2	6.5	3.2
Group 7	1,580.4	138.6	90	2.2	3.9	1.7
China	720.0	64.8	90	1.5	2.3	.8
Zaire	16.4	1.5	90	2.1	2.3	.2
Guinea	3.7	.3	90	2.7	5.4	2.6
India	511.1	46.0	90	2.3	3.4	1.1
Laos	2.8	.3	90	2.4	2.6	.2
Pakistan	120.0	10.8	90	2.7	5.7	2.9
Sudan	14.4	1.3	90	2.9	3.5	.6
Dahomey	2.5	.2	80	2.9	3.8	.9
Mali	4.7	.4	80	2.1	3.3	1.2
Nigeria	61.5	4.9	80	2.6	2.3	− .3
Tanzania	12.2	1.0	80	2.6	4.2	1.6
Afghanistan	15.8	1.1	70	2.0	2.3	.3
Burma	25.8	1.8	70	2.1	3.9	1.8
Chad	3.4	.2	70	1.5	.2	−1.3
Haiti	4.6	.3	70	2.0	1.0	−1.0
Nepal	10.5	.7	70	1.8	2.2	.4
Niger	3.5	.2	70	3.0	2.1	− .9
Yemen	5.3	.4	70	2.1	4.4	2.3
Ethiopia	23.7	1.4	60	2.0	4.3	2.3
Malawi	4.1	.2	60	2.6	3.6	1.0
Rwanda	3.3	.2	60	3.1	2.3	− .8
Burundi	3.3	.2	50	2.0	2.0	.0
Somalia	2.7	.1	50	2.5	4.0	1.5
Upper Volta	5.1	.3	50	2.2	2.3	.1

Source: International Bank for Reconstruction and Development, *World Bank Atlas* (Washington, D.C., 1969 and 1972).

energy than LICs. On the other hand they will gradually become HICs themselves, in the sense that they will have applied a large part of the existing knowledge, and as a consequence further economic development could be expected to slow down somewhat towards the end of the century, irrespective of the energy situation.

The LICs should normally reach stages at which they would have some of the strength of the present MICs. Their economic growth should therefore become faster, but on the other hand most of them will suffer from the higher oil prices. Consequently, only a very slight improvement in performance is foreseen in Assumption 1, but a more important one in Assumption 2.

Food. The description of food consumption contained in Chapter 5 can be expressed in primary calories, a common denominator for vegetable and animal food. It indicates the number of vegetable calories needed for direct human consumption and for feeding the animals from which we get part of our food. One gram of animal protein is calculated as corresponding on the average to 20 calories of animal food. It is further assumed that on the average 7 calories of feeding crops are needed to produce one calorie of animal food. One gram of animal protein therefore corresponds to 140 primary calories.

As an example, the daily food consumption per person in Group 6 (Table 5.9) which is 2,120 calories, including 10 grams of animal protein, corresponds to the following number of primary calories:

Animal food, 10 grams protein	1,400
Vegetable food	1,920
Total	3,320

Since 10 grams of animal protein represent 200 calories of animal food, there remains 1,920 calories to represent vegetable food.

For the year 2000 the assumption is made that the relationships between income levels and food consumption will be approximately the same as in 1967. Since HICs and MICs will have higher income levels in the year 2000 than any of the categories had in 1967, estimates are made by comparison with individual countries with particularly high levels of food consumption in 1967.

THORKIL KRISTENSEN, a professor of economics, is director of the Institute for Future Research and president of the Academy for Research on the Future in Denmark. He is a former Member of Parliament and Minister of Finance in the Danish government, and from 1960 to 1969 he was Secretary-General of the Organization for Economic Cooperation and Development (OECD) in Paris.

Among his many publications are *The Economic World Balance* and *The Food Problem of Developing Countries*.

Dr. Kristensen holds a Dr.sc.pol.h.c. from the University of Ankara.

EUROPEAN DEVELOPMENT POLICIES: The United Kingdom, Sweden, France, EEC, and Multilateral Organizations
Overseas Development Institute
edited by Bruce Dinwiddy

PLANNING FOR DEVELOPMENT IN SUB-SAHARAN AFRICA
Ann Seidman

POTENTIAL EFFECTS OF INCOME REDISTRIBUTION ON ECONOMIC GROWTH: Latin American Cases
William R. Cline

THE UNITED STATES AND THE DEVELOPING WORLD: Agenda for Action, 1974
edited by James W. Howe and the
Staff of the Overseas Development Council

U.S. FOREIGN POLICY AND THE THIRD WORLD PEASANT: Land Reform in Asia and Latin America
Gary L. Olson